YORK HANDBOOKS

GENERAL EDITOR:
Professor A.N. Jeffares
(*University of Stirling*)

AN INTRODUCTION TO LITERARY CRITICISM

Richard Dutton

MA (CAMBRIDGE) PH D (NOTTINGHAM)
*Lecturer in English Literature,
University of Lancaster*

LONGMAN
YORK PRESS

YORK PRESS
Immeuble Esseily, Place Riad Solh, Beirut.

LONGMAN GROUP LIMITED
Longman House,
Burnt Mill,
Harlow,
Essex.

First published 1984
ISBN 0 582 79276 2
Printed in Hong Kong by
Wilture Printing Co Ltd.

Contents

Preface

Much of this Handbook is devoted to surveying the history of literary criticism and chronicling the fortunes of certain texts in that history. These are not offered as something cut-and-dried, to be learned by rote. To know where ideas about literature originated should free us to re-think those ideas for ourselves, and go beyond them; a sense that even the most profound concepts and deeply-felt opinions were in large part shaped by the era that produced them should free us to formulate new concepts and opinions. It is appropriate, therefore, that our advice to those just starting out on the practice of literary criticism should begin with a consideration of what Plato, Aristotle and all their most illustrious successors have written on the subject.

legacy - something handed down
elude - avoid

Part 1

Introduction

A Cinderella subject

The idea that literature is a proper subject for study, because of what it tells us about man himself and about the ways in which he communicates, is for us a legacy of the Renaissance, one of the rediscovered ideas of the classical past. But Renaissance study of literature took many forms: it was studied by philologists, who were primarily interested in it for what it could tell them about the nature of language; it was studied by rhetoricians for its demonstrations of the arts of eloquence and persuasion; it was studied by moral philosophers, who were interested in literature for the bearing it might have on human conduct; it was studied by historians for the records of the past it contained; it was studied by scholars who were concerned to establish accurate texts of the classics and often also what was known of the authors and of the circumstances in which they wrote. The subject which we now call *literary criticism* – which can be provisionally defined as 'the understanding and appreciation of literary texts' – evolved slowly from a combination of these various approaches, prompted largely by Renaissance authors who looked for explanations and justifications for what they themselves were writing. At this time, philology, rhetoric and the rest were all eminently respectable fields of study, firmly established in the educational theory of the day, clearly defined in their terms of reference and (for the most part) in their methods of enquiry. Literary criticism, by contrast, did not have the same respectability and was regarded from the start with some suspicion since it involved picking and choosing among various intellectual approaches, was imprecise about its aims, and was always liable to be dismissed as a medium through which a critic might seek merely to justify his own preferences and prejudices.

Nevertheless, criticism flourished and acquired something of a glamour which has generally eluded the staider disciplines from which it evolved, and this has only increased suspicions that it is really a Cinderella subject: flashy, attractive to some very influential people, but with suspect credentials which might evaporate if midnight ever came. The earliest critics in English were able to point to the eminent examples of Plato (*c.*427–348BC), Aristotle (394–322BC) and Horace (65–8BC) before them, but this was not sufficient to allay the doubts. When British universities first began the study of English as a subject in its own right, about a century ago, many of them (notably Oxford and London) laid a much greater stress on the old disciplines of philology and textual scholarship than they did on literary criticism. Even today, many academic critics feel disturbed by what they perceive as the lack of any agreed aims or methodology in the subject and have looked to such cognate disciplines as linguistics and anthropology to provide them with 'intellectual rigour'.

It is not difficult to see why such doubts should persist. In one form or another criticism has existed almost as long as literature itself (though not separated out as a subject in itself until much later), but its record is dogged by a failure to reach any definitive conclusions either about literature or about its own proper procedures. When Homer invokes 'the divine Muse' or 'the Goddess of Song' to help him to write *The Odyssey* or *The Iliad* he is implicitly making a critical statement about the kind of poem he is composing, about its truth and about its value. He modestly plays down his own role as an author, presenting himself as a kind of agent through whom the tales of the ancient heroes will be enshrined in poetry. It follows that the tales themselves are not mundane, factual histories but share something of the divine truth in their depiction of reality; this explains and justifies the epic mode of the poems, their sheer size and consistently elevated style. It would be difficult to say that Homer is actually *wrong* in this account of his own poems (literary criticism would doubtless be less suspect if we *could* say such things) but it is clear that the arguments he uses carry little weight today – hardly anyone these days would try to justify literature by appealing to the Muses (though see Robert Graves's brilliant if quirky book, *The White Goddess*, revised edition 1961, for evidence that even the oldest theories of literature are not beyond reviving). Nor need our objections stop there; the fact is that Homer's critical premises only apply to one rather limited kind of literature – the kind he is trying to write – and therefore must be construed as special pleading.

Much early English criticism falls under the same heading, deriving from the desire of authors to explain and justify what was new and special in their own writings. See, for example, the prologues to Ben Jonson's (c. 1573–1637) plays; the prefaces to John Dryden's (1631–1700) plays; John Bunyan's (1628–88) 'Apology' for the first part of *The Pilgrim's Progress*; Henry Fielding's (1707–54) preface to *Joseph Andrews*; William Wordsworth's (1770–1850) preface to the *Lyrical Ballads*. In each case we find a piece of special pleading which only applies fully to the particular work it seeks to justify and which, by and large, later generations have found unsatisfactory, preferring to substitute their own reasons for admiring these works (or not, as the case may be). What kind of discipline is it that can allow such apparently limited, partial and transitory judgements?

The partiality of critical judgements cannot, moreover, simply be ascribed to the eagerness of authors to justify their own works; supposedly more objective practitioners of the art of criticism have proved similarly wayward in their judgements. The great fluctuations that have taken place in the reputations of certain writers are a fair indication of how vulnerable the business of literary criticism is: John Donne (1572–1631) and John Webster (c.1580–1625), for example, currently enjoy reputations which would have seemed extraordinary to most of the critics who wrote about them for two centuries after their deaths; Jane Austen (1775–1817), John Keats (1795–1821) and Herman Melville (1819–91) raised little critical excitement during their lifetimes (and what little they did was often hostile); at the other extreme, the dramatists Francis Beaumont (c.1584–1616) and John Fletcher (1579–1625) and the poet Abraham Cowley (1618–67) once enjoyed enormous reputations which are virtually inexplicable to us today. It would be foolish to suppose that the great increase in critical activity over recent years and the supposedly more sophisticated approaches that have been pioneered are going to stop this inexorable process of reputations being revised – any more than they are going to impose a uniform methodology on the subject or lead to some consensus about its aims. This being the case, it is not difficult to see why so many people regard literary criticism as a Cinderella subject.

The real question, however, is whether any of this matters, whether it is significant that we cannot look to criticism for the kind of hard-and-fast answers that we do in, say, chemistry or mathematics. This book is dedicated to the proposition that it does *not* matter, that it is quite appropriate that literary criticism should offer a diversity of approaches and opinions, which will all need to be re-examined from time to time – indeed that it would be quite unhealthy if this diversity and fluidity ceased to exist (as it has, for example, under various authoritarian regimes).

Questions and answers

When Homer appealed to the Muses, and Jonson, Dryden and the others wrote their prefaces, they all tried to answer the two primary questions of literary criticism, which we may baldly pose as:

> *why does a piece of literature have the precise characteristics (form, style, and so on) that it does?* (This question may also be posed, if we accept that there is an analogy between literature and machines, in the form *how exactly does it work?*)

and

> *what is the value of literature, or of a particular piece of literature?*

Inasmuch as our criticism attempts to answer the first question, it may be said to register how we *understand* (a piece of) literature; and inasmuch as it attempts to answer the second, it may be said to register how we *appreciate* it. Whenever those two words are used in this book, they allude to these two basic questions.

Historically, the appreciation of literature has often been seen as the primary issue, engaging critics as diverse as Plato, Sir Philip Sidney (1554–86), Matthew Arnold (1822–88), George Orwell (1903–50) and F. R. Leavis (1895–1978) in attempts to define the central role of literature in our culture as a whole. But Aristotle himself led the way in insisting that the former question, though apparently more limited and technical in scope, might be equally important, and it is usually the one which predominates when literary criticism is taught in schools and universities. All those stock assignments which students will recognise, such as 'Discuss Wordsworth's use of imagery in *The Prelude*' or 'Analyse the narrative structure of *Wuthering Heights*', are really particular examples of the question *how does it work*? Such assignments do, however, tacitly introduce the students to value-judgements; to be asked to comment on *The Prelude* or *Wuthering Heights* inevitably implies that these works will be more interesting or rewarding (in some respects at least) than some possible alternatives. And when a student is asked, for example, to 'Compare Johnson's "The Vanity of Human Wishes" with Gray's "Elegy Written in a Country Churchyard"', it is clear that the teacher does not only look for a comparison of technical details (understanding) but expects an estimate of the relative strengths and weaknesses (appreciation) of the two poems. The fact is that every attempt to *understand* literature carries with it certain value-judgements, while any attempt to *appreciate* literature must carry with it some assumptions about how it 'works'; the two questions overlap, and that is what gives literary criticism as a subject its coherence.

If, then, literary criticism endeavours to answer the two overlapping questions – *what is the value of literature*? and *how does it work*? – it should not be difficult to appreciate why it does not deal in definitive answers. Each question separately is fraught with imponderables, while the two together pose impossible difficulties. Any discussion of value inevitably invokes religious, ethical, political and aesthetic considerations, while any answer to the question of how literature 'works' must first concern itself with the problem of how human beings communicate at all. Any critic worth his or her salt has worked out a position in respect of these issues, but it would be a foolish or a fraudulent critic who claimed to have all the answers: the best we can hope for from any single critical approach is a working hypothesis about such matters, a coherent way of taking as many as possible into account. It is up to us to judge each approach according to its usefulness and effectiveness.

'What is truth?'

'"What is truth?" said jesting Pilate; and would not stay for an answer.'
(Francis Bacon, 'Of Truth'.)

The study of science which, like the study of literature, was revived by the Renaissance has led us to think that there might be – indeed, ought to be – absolute truths about the nature of things, definitive answers to all the questions that face us. In practice we get by quite well without absolute truths, creating working hypotheses for ourselves which we retain until they cease to be useful. So, for example, Ptolemy's hypothesis* about the nature of the universe (that the earth was the centre of the universe and that the sun and the planets revolved around it) was found quite serviceable until that of Copernicus† (the earth revolves around the sun) found greater favour; Copernicus in turn only lasted until Newton‡ (explaining everything according to laws of gravity and motion) appealed more to people's taste; now Newton himself is having to give way to Einstein** (though relatively few people yet understand what Einstein said and make do for most purposes with Newton). Truth, in practice, is the explanation which, for whatever reasons, is most acceptable or most useful to most people at any given time – and it can vary as a result of all kinds of cultural prejudices. We have seen this demonstrated quite forcefully over the last century in the development of a number of 'social sciences' – psychology, anthropology, sociology, linguistics – that have tried to tackle the great questions of human nature, social behaviour and communication in a quasi-scientific manner. In fact they have come no closer to absolute truths than to propose a number of working hypotheses, which we may accept or reject as we find them more or less useful. Their real value, as with any branch of learning, has been to pose the old, imponderable questions in new and exciting ways.

So it has been for literary criticism down the ages, the only real difference being that it has made less pretence than other disciplines of offering final answers. Some critical approaches have been propounded with greater force than others and some – for reasons which have to do with the general cultural climate of the time – have been accepted as virtual orthodoxies for a period; but the subject as a whole – at least in Britain – has been chary of committing itself to absolute dogmas: new ways of asking the old questions have always been open.

*Ptolemy, who flourished in the second century AD, was an Egyptian astronomer and geographer.
†Nicolaus Copernicus (1473–1543), the Polish astronomer.
‡Sir Isaac Newton (1642–1727), the English mathematician and scientist who propounded the concept of universal gravitation and the 'laws of motion'.
**Albert Einstein (1879–1955), the theoretical physicist who propounded the theory of relativity; he worked in Germany, Switzerland and the United States.

The fact is that literature has been valued, indeed often highly valued, in the societies where it has been known; and that it has communicated something to its readers, even if we have not been able to define precisely how or what. Literary criticism makes modest attempts to explain both these facts. This matters because the experience of literature lies at the heart of being the imaginative, creative and social creatures that we are. It would be profoundly disturbing (indeed, in only too many authoritarian countries, it already *is* profoundly disturbing) to be told that only certain lines of enquiry about this experience are allowable, that only certain answers are possible. The uncertainties of literary criticism are a measure of the true variety of imagination and experience, and of the human capacity for change and development.

There is nothing wrong with recent attempts to establish more precise and systematic procedures in literary criticism by importing concepts from the 'social sciences': given the working hypotheses about man and society which are currently fashionable, criticism would lie open to the charge of being moribund if it did not expand in these directions (just as, in the past, it has made reference to such modish disciplines as history and philosophy). It is a measure of the strength of literary criticism, and not of its weakness, that it can accommodate useful insights from other disciplines so readily. It would only be wrong if anyone were to get the idea that these new approaches might totally replace or supersede all others, becoming in some way definitive: 'scientific' orthodoxies about human nature are no more acceptable than political ones. Definitive answers will only come when, for one reason or another, literature ceases to matter any more.

Caveats and consequences

While it has been argued that a wide diversity of approaches to literature is both possible and desirable, it has not been suggested that 'anything goes' in literary criticism, or that any one opinion on literature is as good as any other. True criticism offers itself in a spirit of debate, as a *reasoned* response to one or other of the primary questions with which it concerns itself, as a thoughtful contribution to the understanding and appreciation of literature. Of course this will be coloured by personal tastes and prejudices, but in the last resort we must say that *the reasoned statement matters more than the preferences which it defends.* It is only in spelling out a detailed argument that a critic really enters the debate which has been central to our culture for so long.

For this reason the best literary criticism is never out of date, however much its conclusions seem foreign to our taste. To take one famous example: in the Preface to his edition of *The Plays of William Shakespeare* (1765), Samuel Johnson (1709–84) wrote:

In tragedy he often writes, with great appearance of toil and study, what is written at last with little felicity; but in his comic scenes, he seems to produce without labour, what no labour can improve. In tragedy he is always struggling after some occasion to be comic; but in comedy he seems to repose, or to luxuriate, as in a mode of thinking congenial to his nature. In his tragic scenes there is always something wanting, but his comedy often surpasses expectation or desire. His comedy pleases by the thoughts and the language, and his tragedy for the greater part by incident and action. His tragedy seems to be skill, his comedy to be instinct.

To a modern reader, brought up to think (perhaps too casually) that Shakespeare's tragedies are among the highest flights of literature, this cannot but seem perverse and wrong-headed. Only when we examine the passage in the context of Johnson's primary contention that Shakespeare's greatness lies in being 'above all writers, at least above all modern writers, the poet of nature' do we begin to understand how Johnson can have felt this way, and so appreciate that his approach, his method of thinking about literature, is original, powerful and suggestive. There are other parts of the Preface with which we would probably agree, just as readily as we disagree with this (notably Johnson's magisterial rejection of the tyranny of the 'Aristotelian' unities*); but that matters far less than that we appreciate the engaged intelligence of Johnson's approach as a whole, the premises on which he builds his argument. This should give us food for thought in our own understanding and appreciation of Shakespeare.

We should, then, be sparing about borrowing our judgements, either on literature in general or on particular texts, from other critics. We should be looking to their example, not for ready-made judgements or answers, but for approaches and arguments which we may compare with our own – as a way of clarifying and expanding our own thoughts, not as a substitute for them. So when we quote in our own writing from the work of another critic, we should not do it in the fond hope that a famous name will mysteriously add weight to our feeble efforts: we should only do it as a way of making clear how our own approach stands in relation to that of the other critic and as a way of furthering our own argument.

Two things are deliberately implied in everything written up to this point. One is that, in the study of literature generally, there must be room for a study of critical theory and of the history of criticism, independent of the study of particular texts, authors or genres. The other is that there must always be scope for new contributions to the critical debate, even from the most junior practitioners of the art. And

*See below, pp. 23–4, on the unities, and see pp. 46–7 on Johnson's rejection of them.

these two ideas are linked. We do not need to know, at the outset, exactly what Aristotle, say, or Henry James, said about literature; but we should be aware that they contributed to a debate on literary matters which continues to this day. This knowledge in itself can be intimidating, leading us to suppose that so much has been written and thought down the ages that there is nothing new left to say; but properly understood it should have the opposite, liberating effect. It should lead us to appreciate that there is always a place for a fresh and honest response to any text or question – however limited in range and inarticulate that response may initially be. There is no point in looking to the critics on the library shelves for the 'answer' to your essays and assignments. You should find help and encouragement there, but your answers must, by definition, be your own if they are to be of any value to the critical debate. Once that is understood, it should be apparent that there is nothing inherently impossible or perverse about the idea of writing yet another essay on, say, *Hamlet*, *Paradise Lost* or *Wuthering Heights*.

Part 2

An outline history of literary criticism

IN MUCH OF WHAT FOLLOWS we shall be discussing *poets* and *poetry* where a modern reader might expect to use the broader terms, *author* and *literature*. There is a reason for this. The English word 'poetry' derives ultimately from the Greek verb for 'to make': the poet is a 'maker' and 'poetry' is 'a thing made'. Only gradually were the terms limited in their application to literature, and then specifically to literature in verse. So, for example, Sir Philip Sidney insists in his *Apology for Poetry* (*c*.1580) that 'it is not rhyming and versing that maketh poesy. One may be a poet without versing, and a versifier without poetry', while as late as 1856 the influential art critic John Ruskin (1819–1900) felt able to use the term 'poetry' to mean the creative arts generally. Until the rise of the novel in the early eighteenth century, the greater part of imaginative literature had actually been written in verse, so that, even though the modern use of the terms was beginning to emerge, there was little incongruity about using the term 'poetry' to cover all significant writing (though it was sometimes necessary to make a special point of acknowledging that prose works such as Plato's dialogues and certain section of the Bible were comprehended in the term). Even drama was included in poetry, though it was generally recognised as having special characteristics; Aristotle's *Poetics* (see below, pp. 19–24) is mainly concerned with tragic drama, while Ben Jonson invariably described his plays (including those in prose) as 'poems'.

Bear in mind, therefore, that any criticism of 'poetry' written before approximately 1800 may be understood as criticism of creative literature in general. Plato's strictures against the poets in *The Republic*, for example, should be taken seriously by modern dramatists *and* novelists *and* poets, as well as by critics.

Plato	*c*.427–348 BC

The systematic study of literature in Europe begins with the writings of Plato. This has been an embarrassment to the champions of literature ever since because the great philosopher intended to exclude poets (with only a few minor exceptions) from his ideal Republic. In the long run, however, it may be said that Plato did imaginative literature and literary criticism a favour by being so antagonistic in *The Republic*. All subsequent thinkers on the subject have had to be on their mettle, taking nothing for granted. (Later writers have often tried to hide their embarrassment about Plato's opposition by pointing to the paradoxical discrepancy between what he says about poets and the 'poetic' qualities of his own writing.)

No single work of Plato's is wholly concerned with literature as such. It is a topic on which he touches repeatedly throughout his career, in connection with other more primary concerns – education, morality, theology, metaphysics. As a result it is difficult to abstract a single coherent theory of literature from his writings; his views developed and changed in the course of his career, while certain aspects of literature perhaps received disproportionate treatment as a result of the context in which they were discussed. Nevertheless, he is consistently preoccupied with the ways in which poets misrepresent reality and offer bad moral guidance to their readers.

Plato argues his case most forthrightly in *The Republic*. In it he is primarily concerned with the education which will be necessary for those who are to act as Guardians in his ideal commonwealth.* He is aware that poetry can be attractive to young minds and therefore influential upon them; therein lies its danger. Towards the end of Book 2 and the beginning of Book 3 he catalogues the problem; taking as his premise that God (or the gods – the terms are virtually interchangeable) is by definition all perfect, and therefore neither changes nor practises deceit, he attacks poets for suggesting otherwise:

> any poet who writes about the sufferings of Niobe . . . or the distress of the house of Pelops, or of the Trojan war or any similar subject, must not be permitted to say that these are the works of God . . . he must say that what God did was right and just, and that those who suffered were the better for being punished . . . it is most expressly to be denied that God, being good, can be the cause of evil to anyone – this may neither be said nor sung, in either prose or verse, by any person either young or old, if our commonwealth is to be properly governed. Such a story would be impious, injurious and ill-conceived.

Not only is such literature theologically unsound, he argues, but it is also morally harmful; besides the fact that the gods are misrepresented as bringers of evil and discord, their near-relations, the ancient heroes, are depicted most unflatteringly – in Homer's *Iliad* Achilles sulking in his tent, others taking bribes or consumed by lust:

---

*Plato envisaged government by an ideal aristocracy of Guardians who would be philosophers as well as statesmen.

these lies are positively harmful; for anyone hearing them will be less strict about his own shortcomings if he believes that such behaviour is and was typical of the relations of the gods.

Plato's primary concern in all this is the effect of such 'wicked fictions' on the minds of the military élite who will compose his Guardians. He is particularly distressed that the poets have so consistently suggested that the after-world is a gloomy and unattractive place: they must be forbidden to say so, or the future Guardians will hardly be inspired to fight and die for the commonwealth.

The effect on the minds of the Guardians remains central as he shifts the grounds of his attack to the question of *mimesis*, a crucial word for Greek critics which Plato firstly uses in the specialised sense of 'impersonation'. He argues that the poet continually 'impersonates' other people. For example, the poet writes dialogue for characters in plays as if he were those characters, and similarly in epics he renders verbatim the speeches of the heroes; the only exception is the lyric, where he speaks in his own person. When the potential Guardians read aloud from the works of the poets (as Greek education actually required, because this trained pupils in eloquence, a socially useful skill), they will be encouraged in the idea of 'impersonation', including the imperso-nation of evil characters. This is particularly harmful in Plato's ideal commonwealth where individuals will be expected to know and perform their own special roles, and not to interfere with those of other people.

This fear of the deceptiveness of literature is even more prominent when he considers it later in *The Republic*, in the context of metaphysics. *Mimesis* is now used to mean imitation or representation in a much broader sense, the literal copying of reality in both literature and the visual arts. Plato argues that this is a futile and misleading pursuit because of the nature of reality itself and of our limited perception of it. Since, according to his famous Theory of Ideas or Forms, everything that exists in this world is an imperfect copy of an 'ideal' object that exists outside the substance and time-scale of the world as we perceive it, the creations of poets and artists, being mere copies of copies of 'ideal' reality, are third-hand distortions of truth, valueless and indeed potentially misleading. The example he actually uses is of a bed: God created the 'idea' of the bed; the carpenter creates an actual bed from his imperfect perception of the 'idea'; the poet or artist only produces a superficial imitation of the carpenter's bed, not even knowing anything about the practical skills that went into making it, much less about the 'idea' that lies behind it. The poet or artist offers us verbal or visual versions of the bed, pandering to our senses which are, he insists, the lowest forms of apprehension; this is less satisfactory even than the practical reality of the carpenter's bed and infinitely far-removed from the intellectual truth of the 'idea' of the bed. For Plato, the highest truth is austere, mathematical, intellectual; poetry does not deal in such truth and may positively distract us from it. Indeed, he is generally sceptical about any representation or discussion of reality (and this would include a poem) which is fixed and settled forever; following his master, Socrates, he prefers the fluid, open-ended form of the dialogue or debate as the best way of approaching that approximation to truth which is all we are really capable of achieving.

In an earlier dialogue, the *Ion*, his principal speaker, Socrates, offered the conventional defence of the poet as a man inspired (this is essentially the same argument that we find in Homer): 'the poet is . . . a holy creature and he cannot compose until he has been inspired and has lost his senses . . . the poet does not sing by art but by the divine power [of the Muse]'. Later writers such as Sidney and Percy Bysshe Shelley (1792–1822), who were generally enthusiastic about Plato's philosophy but disappointed by most of what he had to say about poetry, tried to construe this as a chink in his armour: far from being a mere copier of reality at distant removes, the poet is blessed with a divine insight into the highest truth. This, however, is to miss the irony with which Socrates goes on to treat these claims to 'divine' inspiration. In the course of the dialogue he manages to establish that, for all their inspiration, poets are very inefficient conveyors of information – they know less about charioteering than charioteers, less about piloting a ship than its captain, and so on. Inspiration is closer to madness than to real knowledge; it is irrational and therefore a poor guide either to men's conduct or to their understanding. Hence the heavy irony in Book 3 of *The Republic*, when Plato finally decrees that the poets will have to be excluded:

> so, when one of these poets who is able to mimic so many other people and represent all sorts of things comes to our commonwealth, and offers to exhibit both himself and his poetry to us, we will show him all the respect and reverence that is due to such a holy and pleasure-giving person; but we will also have to tell him that the likes of him are not allowed in our state, under the law. So we shall anoint him with myrrh and crown him with garlands, and send him elsewhere.

Divine inspiration is all very well in its way and may be accorded its traditional deference, but it has no place in a sane and well-ordered society. Plato does not, in fact, exclude *all* poets from his Republic: in the interests of educating his Guardians he would admit those who are 'severe' rather than 'entertaining'. In a later work, the *Laws*, he spells out what he has in mind: men not under fifty who have performed noble and virtuous service for the state and will be able to speak to the young with conviction about such matters, if perhaps with little eloquence: 'let their poems be sung, even though they be not very musical.' But even their poetry shall be subject to the censorship of the educators of the Guardians.

Plato's approach to poetry is strictly utilitarian. He demonstrates in numerous examples which there has not been space to quote that he appreciates the power and attraction of 'divinely-inspired' poetry, such as that of Homer and Hesiod:* the more he appreciates it, the more he distrusts it. Hence the ambivalence of the passage in which he finally excludes the poets from the Republic. Given his political concerns, he is mainly interested in the *content* of literature and its effects on audiences, particularly young and impressionable ones: that which enhances the state and its aims will be admitted; anything which does not, or may positively undermine the state, will not. He is interested in the *composition* of literature only inasmuch as it affects the production of responsible poetry: inspiration is, by definition, irresponsible. He is scarcely interested at all in the *form* of poetry, except inasmuch as some forms – drama, for instance – entail more misleading instances of *mimesis* than others: this is perhaps the most vulnerable feature of his approach. He talks as if the mere presentation of untrustworthy gods and fallible heroes will have a corrupting influence on the audience, without asking whether this untrustworthiness might not be put into proper perspective by the work as a whole. Is a work really immoral because it depicts some immoral people? At the other extreme, Plato will admit responsible, by which he means politically acceptable, poems 'even though they be not very musical': again, it is assumed that desired effects can be achieved by the *content* of a poem without regard to its form and technical qualities. We may feel that uninspiring exhortations to virtue and patriotism are positive disincentives, and worse than no exhortations at all.

There is no skating around the fact that Plato's approach to literature, as to most things, is strictly authoritarian. In the interests of a supposedly benign but strictly regulated oligarchy he would sacrifice the creativity and freedom of art. Doubtless Plato did not envisage modern totalitarian regimes, with their ruthless censorship of literature, but the parallels between their ways of thinking on the matter and his are too disturbing to be ignored.

Aristotle   394–322BC

Aristotle's *Poetics* is the most influential book of literary criticism ever written; the ideas it advances still affect thinking today. But we must rid ourselves of one general misconception: it is not a set of 'rules' about literature, as some of Aristotle's followers in the Renaissance believed. It

*They flourished about the eighth century BC and were, respectively, the earliest Greek epic and didactic poets.

is, rather, a work of investigation and description, undertaken in the same scientific spirit as that in which this man of encyclopaedic learning approached all learning: he is primarily concerned to ask the questions 'what exactly is a piece of literature?, what is its function and what are its constituent parts?' His teacher, Plato, had largely concentrated on the question 'what is the value of literature?'; in many respects the *Poetics* offers a reply to Plato's rejection of the greater part of literature, but only obliquely, since Aristotle chooses to approach literary criticism mainly via its complementary concern, 'how exactly does it work?'

He begins by differentiating between the three main kinds of poetry known to the ancient Greeks – the epic, dramatic poetry (tragic and comic) and dithyrambic or lyric poetry – distinguishing between them, as Plato had, in terms of the kinds of *mimesis* or imitation they offer. All poetry imitates, he argues, though it differs in terms of the form, content and manner of imitation: it imitates men in action (natural history in verse, for example, is not real poetry) and these men are either better or worse than ourselves. The latter point, he suggests, explains the distinction between comedy and tragedy: 'for the aim of comedy is to represent men as worse, that of tragedy as better, than in actual life.' Significantly, Aristotle is not concerned with the metaphysics of *mimesis*, as Plato had been; he is content to observe in a factual way that men are naturally imitative, that they enjoy imitating and learn by imitation. He points out that even the imitation of repulsive things, such as lower animals and corpses, can give us pleasure simply by its minute exactness: in other words, the *content* of literature is not everything; its effect is mediated by the manner of its imitation or representation, its *form*. We do not simply react to *what* we are shown, as Plato rather assumes, but also to *how* we are shown it. On this critical distinction rests the whole of Aristotle's literary theory and his tacit repudiation of Plato.

From this he goes on to outline the development of the major poetic forms and their mimetic powers, including the split into tragedy and comedy of dramatic poetry: 'The more serious-minded (poets) depicted noble actions and the deeds of noble men, while those more trivially inclined wrote about the lower sort of people.' This seems to run against the distinction he has just made between form and content, but he does not pursue the point, merely offering the development as a historical fact. He promises to discuss comedy more fully later, but either he never got round to it or what he wrote has not survived. This is one of the most significant omissions in the history of literary criticism: no other critic of the classical past has anything substantial to say about comedy either. The result has been to foster the impression, which Aristotle clearly never intended, that comedy is an inconsiderable form, unworthy of serious attention. Later, in the Christian era, it was difficult to find apologists for comedy: Jesus wept, we are told, but the Gospels tell us nothing about him smiling. Even today the suspicion remains that comedy is inherently an *inferior* form of literature to most others, which there is no real reason to suppose. Are Aristophanes, Jonson, Molière, Congreve, Sheridan and Oscar Wilde* really inferior dramatists because they chose primarily to write comedy rather than tragedy?

Aristotle himself turns here to his main concern, tragedy, explaining that he has chosen to focus on that rather than epic 'because all the elements of epic are to be found in tragedy, but not all the qualities of tragedy are to be found in the epic.' At the end of the *Poetics* he offers a brief analysis of the epic, but finally concludes that tragedy is the superior form.† Aristotle's definition of tragedy has provoked more response than any other critical passage of comparable length:

> an imitation of an action that is serious, complete and of a certain magnitude; in language embellished with every kind of artistic ornament, the various kinds being found in different parts of the play; it represents men in action rather than using narrative, through pity and fear effecting the proper purgation [or relief – the Greek word is *catharsis*] of these emotions.

What does he mean by 'catharsis'? Books have been written on the subject. It seems likely that Aristotle is implicitly referring to the 'mean' of qualities and behaviour – physical, mental, ethical and social – which is the basis of his discussion of humanity in other works, and suggesting that tragedy helps to keep fear and pity in their due proportions by allowing for a kind of ritual purgation of these emotions.

In a more general context, the concept of 'purgation' is vital, whatever precisely Aristotle meant by it. Plato had attacked much existing poetry because he believed that it excited the emotions indiscriminately, inflaming our senses rather than speaking to our reason. Aristotle puts forward the view, at least in respect of tragedy, that poetry, while exciting the emotions, somehow controls and channels them. If this is true, it might be possible to argue that a good deal of imaginative literature might have beneficial effects in terms of channelling potentially disruptive emotions.

The rest of the definition is hardly less vital, because it begins to spell out the idea that a piece of literature is a thing in its own right, with an identifiable shape and characteristics quite separate from those of the things it imitates or represents. We should not think of literature simply

*Aristophanes (*c*.445–*c*.380BC), the Greek comic and satiric dramatist; Molière (1622–73), the greatest French comic dramatist; William Congreve (1670–1729), the English Restoration comic dramatist; Richard Brinsley Sheridan (1751–1816), the Anglo-Irish politician and dramatist; Oscar Wilde (1854–1900), the Anglo-Irish comic dramatist, novelist and essayist.

†The relative status of epic and tragedy remained a favourite bone of critical contention until about 1800.

in terms of what it represents, but should consider the 'imitation' in terms of the form in which it is embodied. So Aristotle goes on to consider what elements constitute the form of a typical tragedy: plot, character, diction, thought, spectacle, and song. Of these he asserts that 'plot is the most important . . . since tragedy is a representation not of men, but of action and life . . . there could be no tragedy without action, but there could be one without character.' That is, it is what certain individuals do, or what is done to them, that is most significant about tragedy; it would theoretically be possible for these individuals to remain anonymous and only defined to the extent that their participation in the action demanded. The action of the plot, moreover, must be complete in itself, which means that it must have a beginning, a middle and an end; all parts of the action must be equally essential to the whole, so that it would not be possible to remove a part without doing damage to the whole; all the parts must be properly ordered, with an appreciable coherence, and the dramatist will not necessarily achieve this simply because he tells the story of a single person.

These precepts add up to what is usually known as the principle of organic unity in literature. Aristotle himself draws an analogy between a tragedy and a living creature – they are alike inasmuch as they are entities with recognisable characteristics, from which it is not possible to abstract a part without damaging the whole, and approximately similar in shape, size and correlation of parts from one example to another. This is particularly valuable because it underlines that Aristotle is only describing general principles, not laying down laws: he is not insisting that two tragedies must be exactly the same in terms of form, merely that they will have the same kinds of similarities as, say, two cats or two fish.

At this point Aristotle digresses to consider the *kind* of truth that the poet tells in his writing, contrasting him with the historian:

> the difference is that one writes about what has actually happened, while the other deals with what might happen. Hence poetry is more philosophical and deserves more serious attention than history; for while poetry concerns itself with universal truths, history considers only particular facts.

This is not so much a repudiation of history as a circumvention of Plato; where Plato had complained that poets only dealt in reality at several removes and that they knew less about practical realities than the charioteers and ships' captains they described, Aristotle insists that they are dealing in a different kind of truth, 'universal truth', imaginatively speculating on the possibilities of human experience. They do not deal in factual, technical or historical truth – and so do not 'lie' – but in something qualitatively different and, he asserts, better.

With this established he can return to a more technical discussion of form in tragedy: the differences between simple and complex plots, the nature of reversals, discoveries and calamities. When he comes to describe tragic action, he is obliged to consider what sort of central character is likely to be most appropriate. Since the action must inspire fear and pity in the audience he concludes that 'good men should not be depicted passing from general well-being to misery, since . . . this merely disgusts us'; evil men progressing from misery to prosperity are similarly inappropriate, while utterly worthless men falling from prosperity to misery would not inspire sufficient sympathy for the required effect:

> But there remains a mean between these extremes. This is the sort of man who is not conspicuously virtuous or just and whose decline into misery is not caused by vice and depravity, but rather by some flaw or error: a man who enjoys prosperity and an eminent reputation, like Oedipus and Thyestes.

This is picked up by later critics as a definition of the 'tragic hero' (a term Aristotle does not use): a man of some social standing and personal reputation, but sufficiently like ourselves in terms of his weaknesses that we feel fear and pity when a tragic flaw, rather than vice, causes his downfall. We tend today to assume that this downfall includes the death of the hero, though this is not necessarily so in Aristotle's terms. Just as we may generalise about the central character, so we may express the broad requirements for other characters in a tragedy: they should be good, for tragedy shows us men better than we normally are, by contrast with comedy; true to type and social standing (for example, women should not be manly or slaves dominant); lifelike; and consistent. This lays the basis for a theory of decorum in character-depiction which, as with so much else in Aristotle, later writers were to expand and make far more rigid. Aristotle merely observes that it is usual for kings to be kingly, cowards cowardly, and so on.

Aristotle was describing and analysing the best literature that he knew and not, of course, all literature. In terms of tragedy that meant, for him, Sophocles (496–406BC) rather than, for example, the earlier Aeschylus (525–456BC) or the more recent Euripides (484–407BC), and particularly the *Oedipus Tyrannus* (*Oedipus the King*) of Sophocles, which he cites as an example of good tragic form more often than any other work. But, while he recommends Sophocles as a good example to other would-be writers, he never implies that everyone should write exactly as he does or that we may deduce 'rules' from his plays which everyone else should follow. Unfortunately, many later writers assumed that this was his intention and rigidified many of his observations into 'laws'.

The most notorious example of this rigidification was the treatment given to the so-called dramatic 'unities' of time, place and action (or 'manner', as the last unity is sometimes called). Only the last of these can really be ascribed to Aristotle: the principle of organic unity requires that all characters and scenes must make an essential contribution to the all-important plot, while the choice of writing either tragedy or comedy leads us to write about characters who are either better or worse than we are. On both these grounds it would be improper to mingle comic action with tragic, or *vice-versa*, since the unity and integrity of form would be lost. But of time in drama, Aristotle says only that 'tragedy tries for the most part to stay within a single revolution of the sun, or only slightly to exceed it, whereas the epic recognises no limits in the time of its action'; this is only an observation on the usual practice of tragedy and epic respectively, as Aristotle knew them, and in no sense a 'rule'. He has nothing whatsoever to say about the place or setting of a tragedy. He does not, for example, say whether the action must all take place in one locality. Yet the Italian critic, Castelvetro, expounded the 'Aristotelian rules' of the unities of time, place and action in drama in his 1570 edition of *Poetics*. These were very influential, particularly in France, and a source of embarrassment to later English critics, faced with the fact that Shakespeare and most other Elizabethan dramatists had paid no attention to them. See the sections on Dryden and Johnson, below.

Horace   65–8BC

As a literary critic, Horace stands to Plato and Aristotle as Rome so often stood to Greece: less subtle, less concerned with philosophic niceties, more practical and, in many ways, more directly influential. Plato and Aristotle were primarily educationalists, but Horace was a practising poet, writing to impress influential friends and patrons at the imperial court of Augustus. His most significant critical work, now generally known as the *Ars Poetica* (On the Art of Poetry) was written as a verse epistle to one such family, the Pisos, a son of which was apparently an aspiring writer. Horace offers practical advice rather than theoretical propositions, drawing freely on the ideas of earlier writers; he devotes most attention to drama, even though this was not his own field. His tone is that of a more casual Aristotle, though his advice is altogether more dogmatic.

Horace is not much concerned with the conundrums of literature-as-imitation, but has a good deal to say about the respective places of 'nature' and of 'art' in literary composition, laying much the greater emphasis on the latter. On the one hand he asserts that 'the practised poet, as an imitative artist, should regard human life and character as his models, deriving from them a language that is true to life.' In practice, however, the best way of achieving such a language is to imitate the best models of the old Greek writers rather than to experiment on your own. 'You must give your days and nights to the study of Greek models', he says, citing Homer and the great tragedians as the best examples. This is consistently the balance Horace strikes: clearly a poet must be born with some ability, and there will always be scope for originality as long as it follows the dictates of 'nature', but too much originality is dangerous; it leads to obscurity and incoherence, to purple patches that are not properly integrated within the work as a whole – and all these are faults to be avoided. Better stick to the proven models of the past than rely too much on instinct. The poet must work to polish his lines, making them clear and consistent; he must be judicious (the Latin verb, *sapere*, lies somewhere between wisdom and learning in English), guided by discipline and capable of self-criticism.

Central to Horace's insistence on 'art' in poetry is the concept of literary decorum, the fitness and propriety of the form and style of a work to its content. Aristotle touches on features of this, but Horace makes it his guiding principle. Every aspect of a poem must be in keeping with the nature of the work as a whole: the genre must be carefully chosen to fit the subject-matter, and the characters (in narrative and dramatic poetry) must be suitable for the genre, while every feature of expression – style, tone, metre, and so on – must be in keeping. There must be no mixing of genres and nothing implausible in the characterisation or the action (so, for example, a dramatist should keep the use of the *deus ex machina** strictly under control). In this context he lays down that no unnatural violence should be enacted on stage, although Aristotle thought it permissible; such action should be reported rather than depicted, apparently for the sake of plausibility. Later ages were to interpret this rule very strictly.

When Horace considers the purpose of literature, he suggests that 'the aim of poets is to give either profit or delight, or to mix the giving of pleasure with useful precepts for life.' The ideal balance is achieved by 'the man who has contrived to combine profit with delight . . . since he pleases his reader at the same time as he instructs him.' This was such an attractive formulation – allowing literature to be 'delightful' without being merely hedonistic, and 'useful' without being tied to the service of any particular code or dogma – that it has been widely adopted ever since, even by many who do not share Horace's other beliefs.

In the *Ars Poetica*, as elsewhere, Horace talks as a rational man addressing other rational men. Without making exaggerated claims for it, he sees poetry as something that helps to shape an agreeable civilisation, such as the one in which he, a comfortably-off Roman, lived himself. While he never actually claims that *any* educated man can become a poet, the inference does not seem far away: following example,

---

*Literally, the god from the machinery; it comes to mean any providential intervention in the nick of time. Gods or goddesses were let down on to the stage by a device or machine in the Greek and, later, Roman theatres.

following the rules, following decorum – these are far more important than outright originality, and it is not without significance that the epistle ends with some satirical fun at the expense of supposedly mad or 'inspired' poets – such as those whom, for different reasons, Plato was prepared to exclude from his Republic. Aristotle had led the way by demonstrating that poetry was as much a matter of art and technique as it was of inspiration, but it is Horace who translates description into prescription, providing rules of composition which might be part of the education of any gentleman. Where Aristotle observes that a play should be long enough and have the appropriate features to treat its subject in the proper manner, Horace insists on five acts. Where the former describes what Homer has made of the epic, the latter insists that the shape and content of the epic have been *defined* by Homer; since *he* started in mid-action, everyone else must start, in his famous phrase, *in medias res*. And where Aristotle had suggested a principle of decorum about characterisation, Horace has jumped virtually to the point of stereotype: all old men are lazy, live in the past, criticise anything new; all young boys like dogs and horses and open fields; and so on – do nothing to confuse your reader.

Horace has not been very fashionable since the time of the Romantic poets; he makes poetry sound like a mechanical skill rather than a vital art. He is an arch-conservative in an age of intellectual revolutions. But it is fair to say that his advice is sensible and practical even today (if due allowance is made for the literary forms now prevalent) and need not inhibit any genuinely gifted author. In the period 1500–1800 he was by far the most influential of all literary critics: his ideas on decorum, 'delightful teaching' and imitation of classical models lie at the heart of Renaissance literary theory. It is also true to say that no critic demonstrates so readily as Horace the association between critical theory and assumptions about the nature of civilisation in general.

'Longinus'   *c.*1st–3rd centuries AD

We do not know who wrote the treatise traditionally known as *On the Sublime* and traditionally, but incorrectly, ascribed to Cassius Longinus; nor do we know precisely when it was written. To compound our problems the manuscripts are incomplete, with some unfortunate gaps, while the usual English version of the title is misleading: the key Greek term, *hypsos*, does not really mean sublimity as we understand it. Wordsworth was closer to the point when he wrote that 'Longinus treats of animated, impassioned, energetic, or, if you will, elevated writing.' For all that, the treatise is complete enough to be coherent; let us accept the traditional author and title on the understanding that it is the argument which really matters.

Longinus writes as someone for whom his chief interest, the great period of Greek literature, lies well in the past: the great dramatists have all been dead well over three hundred years and Homer a good deal longer than that. He is concerned to define exactly what it is that constitutes the greatness of the established classics and to see if anything can be learned from this to revive literature in his own time. The treatise actually breaks off in the middle of a chapter on 'the decay of eloquence'.

Longinus asserts that 'sublimity' is what marks out true greatness, arguing that

> the sublime consists in a particular excellence and distinction of expression, and that this alone gave the greatest poets and historians their pre-eminence and won for them undying fame. For the effect of animated language is not to persuade the audience but to entrance them. Without exception, what transports us with wonder is more telling in every way than what merely persuades or pleases us.

Unlike Horace, who looks first for competence and consistency, and decries purple passages, Longinus is all for 'a well-timed flash of sublimity [which] scatters everything before it like a bolt of lightning, revealing in a flash the full power of the speaker'.

Such sublimity does not occur by chance, he maintains. The gift of genius may be innate but it must be moulded and trained by, for example, emulation of the sublime writers of the past. In this respect he is surprisingly close to Horace; art can always enhance natural ability. It is not to be expected that any author can be sublime consistently – 'even Homer nodded', as later ages were to remark – but application to the necessary skills will help the author. Longinus parts company with Horace entirely, however, when he makes the assertion that even occasional touches of sublimity are preferable to mere unrelieved competence.

How, then, are we to identify the sublime? How precisely can we define it? Here is Longinus's answer:

> Some inherent quality of the true sublime lifts up our souls: elevated with a sense of proud possession, we are filled with joy, as if we had ourselves produced what we heard. If a sensible and well-read man hears a passage several times and finds that it does not either touch him with a sense of sublimity or leave more food for thought in his mind than the mere words suggest; rather that the more carefully he considers it the less impressive he finds it, then it cannot really be an example of the true sublime . . . . In general terms, you may consider that to be truly beautiful and sublime which pleases all men at all times.

The last sentence reveals the main flaw in Longinus's approach. Does *anything* please all people at all times? Surely not. Can it really be satisfactory to leave it to some putative expert, the ideal reader, 'sensible and well-read', to apply some infallible, but ultimately subjective, test to distinguish the true sublime from the false? Doubtless aware of these problems himself, Longinus devotes much of the treatise to bolstering these dubious contentions by examining many examples of what he would describe as sublimity.

There are, he asserts, five sources of the sublime. Most important is greatness or elevation of thought, the ability to grasp grand conceptions, which is only possible if the author is truly noble of soul. In this context he quotes from Homer and, most strikingly, from the opening passage of the Book of Genesis in the Bible. He also cites as a special example a complete ode by Sappho (*fl. c.*580BC), the Greek lyric poetess. The second source is vehement and inspired emotion, on which he promises a separate treatise and so does not dwell – this has not, in fact, survived. Thirdly, the sublime may derive from effective but unobtrusive use of rhetorical figures. Fourthly, it may be found in 'notable language', including metaphor and other verbal embellishments. Finally, Longinus cites the general dignity and elevation of style as a source of sublimity; this extends from the particular arrangement of the words to the broad structure of the work, where he insists on the well-established concept of organic unity, though it is notably lower on his list of priorities than it is on Aristotle's.

Longinus has never been as influential a critic as the other three we have considered from the classical period, though he did enjoy an understandable vogue with the onset of Romanticism. (William Wordsworth (1770–1850), for instance, was very interested in him). His contention, however, that what matters in literature are its inspired and inspiring moments, its truly memorable passages, is one which many people find attractive (not least when it is coupled with the contention that this 'sublimity' appeals to human beings because they have naturally aspiring minds). The problem, of course, is how we are to reach a consensus on what is sublime and what constitutes sublimity. For all that Longinus tries to defend his assertions by intelligent reference to numerous examples, he never comes up with a formula which is objectively verifiable or universally acceptable – nor, indeed, has anyone else since his time. In the end, we may say that the sheer enthusiasm of *On the Sublime*, coupled with its sensitive response to such a wide variety of texts, matters every bit as much in the history of criticism as its theoretical premise.

The Middle Ages and the Renaissance

Little of significance was added to literary criticism in the period between the fall of Rome in the fifth century and the great rediscovery of the classical past we know as the Renaissance (c.1300–1600 in Italy, though it was rather later in starting in France and England). The crucial development in this period was the adoption of Christianity, and specifically the Christianity of the Church of Rome, as the universal religion of Western Europe. This made all the literature of the classical past automatically suspect, written as it was by pagans or outright atheists (though there were attempts to read some of it allegorically as obliquely relevant to Christian truth; Virgil's* 'Fourth Eclogue' was credited with foretelling the birth of Christ, while his *Aeneid* was interpreted as an allegory of the soul's quest for salvation). There was, moreover, a deep ascetic strain in the leadership of the early Church, which regarded imaginative literature as a potential distraction from higher things, if not indeed a positive incentive to deceit and dishonesty because it 'told lies'. St Augustine† was typical in this respect, ironically borrowing from the 'pagan' Plato's attacks on poetry in his *City of God* (after 410) to warn against the dangers of literature. The sole exception, of course, was the Bible (and the body of patristic, doctrinal and devotional writing which grew up around it). But the Bible was regarded as the word of God; it could not be approached like any other book. Only the clergy were allowed to interpret it, and they only within limits laid down by the hierarchy of the Church.

When the Renaissance came, literary criticism revived firstly in the efforts of writers such as Dante and Boccaccio‡ to justify their own works, which were written in forms unknown to the classical critics. The novelty of form was linked with the question of whether they should write in the vernacular (Italian, French, English) or in the 'universal' language, Latin. After the fall of Constantinople in 1453, many Greek scholars fled to the West, taking their manuscripts with them; this intensified interest in the classical past and gave people a much better understanding, in particular, of Plato, whose works were only imperfectly known before this time. The Renaissance came belatedly to England, which was ravaged by dynastic squabbles known as the Wars

---

*Virgil (70–19BC) was the most respected of all Latin poets. His *Eclogues* are pastoral poems on rural themes; his *Georgics* is a didactic poem on farming; and the *Aeneid* is the epic which links the fall of Troy with the founding of Rome through the person of the Trojan hero Aeneas.

†St Augustine of Hippo (AD354–430) was a leader of the early Christian church; not to be confused with the later St Augustine, first Archbishop of Canterbury.

‡Dante Alighieri (1265–1321), greatest of the Italian poets, author of *The Divine Comedy*, written c.1307–21. Giovanni Boccaccio (1313–75), the Italian humanist, who wrote *The Decameron* (1349–51).

of the Roses for most of the fifteenth century; then, when the arts seemed to be reviving at the Court of Henry VIII, it was thrown into confusion again by the Reformation. Only when a political and religious settlement was secured under Elizabeth I was culture, and literature in particular, able to flourish. Mid-way through her reign, England's literary Renaissance found its perfect spokesman in Sir Philip Sidney.

Sir Philip Sidney   1554–1586

Sidney's critical treatise was written about 1580 but not published until 1595, after his death, when two separate editions were published under different titles, *An Apology for Poetry* and *The Defence of Poesy*. The former title is used in this Handbook. The *Apology* (meaning 'explanation' rather than 'excuse') is scarcely original in anything it says (most of the key ideas are taken from Plato, Aristotle and Horace) but owes its significance to its timing, its spirited style and to the fact that it was written by Sidney. When he wrote it, Sidney was nephew and heir presumptive to the most powerful man in the kingdom, the Earl of Leicester; he was looked to as an ideal embodiment of the Renaissance spirit: courtier, soldier and poet.

It is said that he wrote the *Apology* in response to a work which had been dedicated to him, attacking poetry and plays; the author of this book, Stephen Gosson (1554–1624), was supposedly misled by Sidney's staunchly Protestant and anti-Catholic political associations into believing that he would be sympathetic to Puritan-style attacks on poetry as a frivolous and dangerous distraction. The story may not be true, but if it is, Gosson seriously miscalculated. Sidney puts forward one of the most enthusiastic arguments for poetry ever penned, censuring only its abuse, and giving some suggestions as to how poetry, including drama, may be improved in England: this only a few years before the great works of Spenser (whom he knew), Marlowe, Shakespeare, Donne, Jonson and all the other Elizabethan writers.*

'Poesy', says Sidney, 'is an art of imitation, for so Aristotle termeth it in his word *mimesis*, that is to say, a representing, counterfeiting, or figuring forth; to speak metaphorically, a speaking picture, with this end, to teach and delight.' (The latter formula, of course, derives from Horace rather than Aristotle.) But poetry does not offer a *literal* description of reality (which is why it does not tell lies, as some claim; it does not assert untruths as truths); it offers rather a heightened version of reality: 'Nature never set forth the earth in so rich tapestry as divers

*Edmund Spenser (?1552–99), author of *The Faerie Queene* (1596); Christopher Marlowe (1564–93), poet and dramatist, author of *Doctor Faustus*; William Shakespeare (1564–1616), greatest of English poets and dramatists; John Donne (1572–1631), poet and Dean of St Paul's, whose *Songs and Sonets* are discussed in Part 3.

poets have done; neither with pleasant rivers, fruitful trees, sweet-smelling flowers, nor whatsoever else may make the too-much-loved earth more lovely; her world is brazen, the poets deliver only a golden.' This is true in depictions not only of nature but also of men; he mentions Xenophon's* Cyrus and Virgil's Aeneas as examples of the 'golden' men offered by the poets. On these grounds he compares poetry favourably with history and philosophy, averring that 'the end of all earthly learning being virtuous action, those skills that most serve to bring forth that have a most just title to be princes over all the rest.' In this respect he finds that history is too tied to particular facts, while philosophy is too abstract and obscure, but the poet with his 'golden' fables is ideal:

Now therein of all sciences . . . is our poet the monarch. For he doth not only show the way, but giveth so sweet a prospect into the way as will entice any man to enter into it. Nay, he doth, as if your journey should lie through a fair vineyard, at the very first give you a cluster of grapes, that full of that taste you may long to pass further. He beginneth not with obscure definitions, which must blur the margin with interpretations, and load the memory with doubtfulness. But he cometh to you with words set in delightful proportion, either accompanied with, or prepared for, the well-enchanting skill of music; and with a tale, forsooth, he cometh unto you, with a tale which holdeth children from play, and old men from the chimney-corner; and, pretending no more, doth intend the winning of the mind from wickedness to virtue.

Sidney contrives to answer all those who scorn or hate poetry, including Plato, who, he argues, 'only meant to drive out those wrong opinions of the Deity, (whereof now, without further law, Christianity hath taken away all the hurtful belief) . . . . So as Plato, banishing the abuse, not the thing . . . shall be our patron and not our adversary.' Of course the advent of Christianity, which relegated the stories of the old gods to the same status as any other fable, did not answer all of Plato's objections to poetry, but Sidney glosses over this in his eagerness to have all the most admired classical philosophers on his side.

With so little of consequence yet written by his contemporaries, Sidney is limited in his judgement of particular English works, but it is clear from the few examples he gives which way he was inclined: '[Spenser's] *Shepheardes Calender* [1579] hath much poetry in his eclogues, indeed worthy the reading, if I be not deceived. That same framing of his style to an old rustic language I dare not allow, since neither Theocritus in Greek, Virgil in Latin, nor Sannazzaro in Italian did affect it.' In the drama, he objects 'how all their plays be neither right tragedies nor right comedies, mingling kings and clowns, not because

*Xenophon (c.430–c.350BC) was a Greek soldier, historian and man of letters.

the matter so carrieth it, but thrust in the clown by the head and shoulders to play a part in majestical matters, with neither decency nor discretion'; he admires the 'stately speeches and well-sounding phrases' of Sackville and Norton's* early tragedy, *Gorboduc* (acted 1561; first published 1565), 'full of notable morality', but even that is censured 'for it is faulty both in place and time' – breaking what he believes to be Aristotle's precepts on the unities. Sidney is, in short, a conservative in the Horatian manner, believing in decorum and a proper respect for ancient examples which have stood the test of time. But he is not totally dogmatic. He seems to be prepared to sanction the mingling of kings and clowns if 'the matter so carrieth it' – applying the spirit rather than the law of Aristotle's precepts; it would have been interesting to see what he would have made of Shakespeare's handling of these conventions. Contrary to some modern preconceptions, moreover, Sidney repeatedly demonstrates that Horatian conservatism is not incompatible with a real enthusiasm for poetry as a living force: 'I never heard the old song of Percy and Douglas [the ballad of 'Chevy Chase'] that I found not my heart moved more than with a trumpet'; 'truly, many of such writings as come under the banner of unresistible love, if I were a mistress would never persuade me they were in love; so coldly they apply fiery speeches, as men that had rather read lovers' writings . . . than that in truth they feel those passions.' Perhaps Donne read those words and took them to heart.

Sidney's conviction that poetry matters, that it moves us, is what keeps *An Apology for Poetry* alive. Sidney writes as a man of the world (he mentions his diplomatic missions, for example), for whom poetry has a natural and honoured place in his life. He was an author himself, though his critical work is in no direct sense a justification of his major pieces, the *Arcadia*† and *Astrophel and Stella*;‡ he writes as though his readers will be conversant with poetry and may well also write themselves. This mode of criticism – poets writing as if for potential fellow-poets – survived well into the eighteenth century; the idea that creative artists are likely to be the most knowledgeable critics is not dead even now. The concept that literary criticism may be a fit pursuit for a gentleman, that it should remain a casual, amateur occupation, is peculiarly English and is still reflected in the English reticence about modern American and European critical approaches which are avowedly specialist and 'professional'.

*Thomas Sackville (*c*.1536–1608), later Earl of Dorset and Lord High Treasurer of England, and Thomas Norton (1532–84), poet and Member of Parliament.
†A long romance on courtly themes in both prose and verse, first published in 1590.
‡The most influential of all English sonnet sequences, written *c*.1581, published 1591.

John Dryden	1631-1700

With Sidney dead, no contemporary critic attempted a full assessment of the achievement of the great period of Elizabethan and Jacobean writing: an omission which much later criticism has been concerned to make good. Ben Jonson (c.1573-1637) came closest, with prologues and inductions to many of his plays, his common-place book (*Timber, or Discoveries*) and some off-the-cuff remarks about his contemporaries which happen to have survived; he was essentially Horatian in outlook, insisting on decorum, reasonable standards of craftsmanship and mixing 'delight' with 'profit'. John Milton (1608-74) defended poetry during the Commonwealth period, when Puritan attacks on literature (particularly on the theatre) were most virulent; against accusations that most literature was either frivolous or immoral or implicitly monarchist in its sympathies, Milton argued for a poetry that was fiercely moral, based largely on the Bible; freedom-loving, in a responsible, middle-class style of freedom, abhorring both the tyranny of kings and the licence of the mob; and patriotic, in celebrating the progress of a pious nation towards God's goals. But it was not until Dryden's *Essay of Dramatic Poesy* (1668) that England produced another major critical treatise.

The *Essay* only came to be written because the Great Plague of 1665 closed the theatres in London. Cut off from his most lucrative literary employment, Dryden retired to the country, where he produced what in effect is an extended version of the play prefaces which had been pioneered by Jonson in England and Corneille* in France; Dryden himself had already used one for his first printed play, *The Rival Ladies* (1664), and was to continue using them throughout his career. The *Essay of Dramatic Poesy* is different in that it was not attached to any particular play and is dressed up as a fictitious dialogue between four characters, ostensibly weighing up the relative merits of various forms of drama; but it is clear that Dryden's main interest, here as elsewhere, lies in justifying the kind of plays with which he was most concerned at the time – this happened to be rhymed heroic drama – rather than in dispassionate analysis. This is reflected in the setting of the dialogue; it is Dryden's contention that rhymed heroic drama is the supreme achievement of the native dramatic tradition and a true reflection of the standards of taste set by the Restoration, so the characters are placed in a boat on the Thames (a gentlemanly way to travel) and can hear the noise of a naval battle – an English victory over the Dutch in June 1665 – in the far distance, an occasion for patriotic pride and satisfaction.

*Pierre Corneille (1606-74), French dramatic poet, creator of French neoclassical tragedy; author of *The Cid* (c.1637).

The *Essay* opens with a lively and convincing discussion that throws up a rough-and-ready definition of a play: 'A just and lively image of human nature, representing its passions and humours, and the changes of fortune to which it is subject, for the delight and instruction of mankind.' The lack of precision here reflects Dryden's lack of interest in theoretical or abstract considerations throughout; the Horatian pieties ('delight and instruction') place no real constraints on his efforts to demonstrate – with all the insight and conviction of a practising dramatist – that some forms of drama work more satisfactorily than others, and this is his main concern. After the apparent spontaneity of the opening, the *Essay* settles into six set speeches, arranged in three pairs, with no real attempt at credible dialogue: Crites defends ancient dramatic practice, Eugenius that of the Moderns; Lisideus speaks in favour of recent French drama and Neander ('the new man', probably Dryden himself) defends the English; Crites advances the claims of blank verse, and Neander those of rhyme. In each case the second speaker carries more conviction, partly because he has the opportunity to refute his opponent's propositions. So Crites argues in favour of the pseudo-Aristotelian unities, but Eugenius is able to point to many instances where classical writers disobeyed their own 'rules', indeed that the 'rules' are a spurious later invention; furthermore,

> we own all the helps we have from them, and want neither veneration nor gratitude ... but to these assistances we have joined our own industry; for, had we sat down with a dull imitation of them, we might then have lost somewhat of the old perfection, but never acquired any that was new.

As modern science has gone beyond Aristotle, so may modern drama go beyond the example of the ancients, not least in making good the ancients' notable failure to write plays with love as a central theme. Dryden, incidentally, was a founder-member of the influential Royal Society, which flourishes to this day. It was dedicated to the 'advancement' of both science and language, on lines laid down by Francis Bacon (1561–1626), the lawyer, essayist, politician and philosopher of science, author of *The Advancement of Learning* (1605). The Society was instrumental in persuading authors to adopt a simpler prose style, 'a close, naked way of speech', according to Thomas Sprat (1635–1713), Bishop of Rochester and the first historian of the Society.

Lisideus argues in favour of the French dramatists mainly on the grounds that, in the well-regulated culture developed under Cardinal Richelieu* (by contrast with the confusion of the English Civil War),

---

*Cardinal Duc de Richelieu (1585–1642), a powerful French statesman who founded the Académie Française, which attempted to regulate French language and literature on strictly authoritarian lines.

they had followed classical rules and precedents more closely than the English. Neander counters – in what, for us, is probably the most interesting part of the *Essay* – by urging that the dramatists of Elizabethan England have more variety in their plays and so imitate life more closely; tragi-comedy, to which Lisideus had taken particular exception, allows comedy to heighten the pathos of tragedy by contrast and is simply more entertaining for the audience. (Here Dryden writes out of his professional experience as a dramatist.) He tries to demonstrate this in respect of particular individuals:

> To begin, then, with Shakespeare. He was the man who of all modern, and perhaps ancient poets, had the largest and most comprehensive soul. All the images of nature were still present to him, and he drew them, not laboriously, but luckily; when he describes anything, you more than see it, you feel it too . . . . He is many times flat, insipid; his comic wit degenerating into clenches [puns], his serious swelling into bombast. But he is always great, when some great occasion is presented to him.

He briefly considers Beaumont and Fletcher, who remained remarkably popular in the Restoration ('two of theirs being acted through the year for one of Shakespeare's or Jonson's'), paving the way in many respects for Dryden's own heroic drama. Then he turns to Jonson, whom he considers

> the most learned and judicious writer which any theatre ever had . . . . If I would compare him with Shakespeare, I must acknowledge him the more correct poet, but Shakespeare the greater wit. Shakespeare was the Homer, or father of our dramatic poets; Jonson was the Virgil, the pattern of elaborate writing; I admire him, but I love Shakespeare.

Neander/Dryden consistently has his cake and eats it too: he loves Shakespeare, the natural genius, admires Jonson as the perfect example to follow, and yet acknowledges that Beaumont and Fletcher outdo both of them when it comes to pleasing contemporary audiences. And somehow each of these, in his different way, helps to prove the English superior to the French.

In this eclectic spirit Neander tries to clinch his case for the English dramatists with a detailed *examen*, as he calls it, of Jonson's play, *The Silent Woman* (or *Epicoene**). This is the first extended critical analysis of a single work in English; it is uneven and unsatisfactory but undoubtedly breaks new ground. He tries to demonstrate that the play actually abides by the three 'unities', even though earlier he had

---

*This play of 1609 is a comedy of 'humours', exploring the moral and psychological foibles of fixed character-types.

suggested that they did not matter so much and though he has to distort
the facts to do it: he ignores some of the indicated settings of the play in
order to claim that it has unity of place and has to overlook a number of
disparate scenes in order to make the claim that 'the action of the play is
entirely one; the end or aim of which is the settling Morose's estate on
Dauphine'. He is clearly uncomfortable about Morose as a central
character, who is so averse to noise as to seem unbelievable; firstly he
tries to claim that Jonson actually knew such a person but then he goes
on to demonstrate that he understands well enough the artistic theory of
'humours' on which the characterisation is really based.

He is, however, much sounder when he comes to analyse the plot,
commenting that

> the business of it rises in every act. The second is greater than the first;
> the third than the second; and so forward to the fifth . . . and when the
> audience is brought into despair that the business can naturally be
> effected, then, and not before, the discovery is made. But that the poet
> might entertain you with more variety all this while, he reserves some
> new characters to show you . . . all which he moves afterwards in by-
> walks, or under-plots, as diversions to the main design, lest it should
> grow tedious, though they are still naturally joined with it, and
> somewhere or other subservient to it.

Thus the play is exciting and entertaining, abides by the unity of action
but also offers the audience variety. We may feel, however, that the case
would have been more convincing if he had shown *how* some of the lesser
characters are 'naturally joined' with the main design.

All in all, Dryden reveals himself to be a pragmatic or liberal neoclassical critic. His discussions are naturally cast in terms of Aristotelian
'rules' and Horatian doctrine, but common sense and experience teach
him that there are exceptions, some of them dictated by the irrefutable
will of the audience: classical precedent is all very well as a starting-
point, but the moderns must be free to improve upon it when the
situation demands. Shakespeare breaks many of the 'rules' but there is a
greatness in him which Dryden insists on recognising even though he
cannot define it very precisely; Beaumont and Fletcher may not write
perfect plays but they are very popular, and Dryden is professional
enough to recognise that this is vital. Much of what he says is tinged with
a Restoration* conviction that England has reached new heights of
civility and culture, enabling her to go beyond the ancient classics, the
French who slavishly imitate them and even her own literary giants of
the last generation who – for all their innate genius, variety and ability to

---

*A term applied to the literature and culture of the period (approximately 1660–1700)
after Charles II was restored to the English throne. It is characteristically a period of
patriotic self-assurance.

please the audience – all too often lacked the refinement of taste enjoyed by the gentlemen of the Restoration. The modern English dramatist is free to draw on the best examples, wherever they come from, as for instance to follow the French in the use of rhyme in heroic drama: 'Tragedy, we know, is wont to image to us the minds and fortunes of noble persons, and to portray these exactly; heroic rhyme is nearest nature, as being the noblest kind of modern verse.' It is typical of Dryden's pragmatism that, ten years later, he was able to turn round and argue in favour of blank verse, in the preface to *All for Love* (1678): 'Not that I condemn my former way, but that this is more proper to my purpose.'

Criticism for Dryden is the justification of whatever *works*, however much he may dress it up by invoking neoclassical 'rules' and 'authorities'; occasionally, he gets very close to admitting that what may work in one time and place may not be so effective in another: 'though nature . . . is the same in all places, and reason too the same, yet the climate, the age, the disposition of the people, to which a poet writes may be so different, that what pleased the Greeks would not satisfy an English audience.' But Dryden goes no further than this; in common with virtually all his contemporaries, he has to start from the assumption that universally-valid 'rules' of composition exist, even if experience prompts us from time to time to bend them. It is worth reviewing the *examen* of *The Silent Woman* in this light: the first extended piece of 'practical criticism' in English is far from being a dispassionate analysis of the text. It is, on the contrary, a highly partial account of the play in the light of strong presuppositions about what is proper and what 'works' in comic drama. This is not to condemn Dryden or to say that he is wrong in his criticism, merely to acknowledge that he belongs to a particular time and a particular culture. We should beware of assuming that later examples of 'practical criticism' are in fact any more dispassionate, however much more sophisticated they appear to be.

Alexander Pope   1688–1744

Pope's *An Essay on Criticism* is the only significant critical treatise in English written in verse; it is famous for its polished lines, many of which have become proverbial ('A *little learning* is a dangerous thing'; 'For fools rush in where angels fear to tread'; 'To err is human, to forgive, divine') but it cannot lay claim to great distinction as a contribution to critical thought. It is the work of a precocious young man (written *c.*1705–9, published 1711), keen to display his talent but with little that is really new or profound to say.

The key term in Pope's *Essay* is 'Nature':

First follow Nature, and your judgement frame
By her just standard, which is still [that is, always] the same.

(lines 68-9)

This is not Nature as the Romantics were to understand it, wild and mysterious, but something reflecting deep order, moderation, universal laws; it places due limits on men's taste and writing, dictating that they should avoid excesses of enthusiasm and freakish originality. The precepts of the great classical thinkers were based on Nature, and so valuable for that reason:

Those RULES of old discovered, not devis'd,
Are Nature still, but Nature methodiz'd;
Nature, like liberty, is but restrain'd
By the same laws which first herself ordain'd.

(lines 88-91)

Look at Virgil, he says, inspired with great ambition and boundless talent:

Perhaps he seem'd above the critic's law,
And but from Nature's fountains scorn'd to draw:
But when t'examine ev'ry part he came,
Nature and Homer were, he found, the same.

(lines 132-5)

Pope seems to be addressing poets and critics equally in spelling out the criteria of good taste; past precept and past example are to be respected not simply for their antiquity but because they enshrine Nature's laws. This is a recipe for restraint, moderation ('avoid extremes') and common sense which, he argues, calls for precisely the kind of poetry he himself writes. The old Metaphysical style (see the section on Donne's *Songs and Sonets* in Part 3) of Donne and Cowley had been lively and flamboyant but artless in its disregard of Nature:

True Wit is Nature to advantage dress'd,
What oft was thought, but ne'er so well express'd.

(lines 297-8)

Poetry and its appreciation is still, for Pope, the business of an educated gentleman, as it had been for Sidney; what distinguishes the Augustans is a conviction that they have achieved a level of taste and civility far beyond that of their Renaissance predecessors, so that Pope looks for poets/critics 'Though learned, well-bred; and though well-bred, sincere'.

This confident superiority is best reflected in the closing portions of the *Essay*, where Pope offers a history of literary criticism: the great critics of the classical past had 'methodiz'd' Nature, suppressed 'licence' and brought a golden age; this was obliterated by the Dark Ages, but the Renaissance started a slow progress back to the old standards:

> But Critic-learning flourish'd most in France:
> The rules a nation, born to serve, obeys;
> And Boileau still in right of Horace sways.
> But we, brave Britons, foreign law despis'd,
> And kept unconquer'd, and unciviliz'd;
> Fierce for the liberties of wit, and bold,
> We still defy'd the Romans, as of old.
> Yet some there were, among the sounder few
> Of those who less presum'd, and better knew,
> Who durst assert the juster ancient cause,
> And here restor'd Wit's fundamental laws.

(lines 712–22)

Pope contrives not only to sneer at the seventeenth-century French for being over-deferential to the neoclassical 'rules' (expressed with the strictest orthodoxy by Boileau*), but also to poke fun at the English insularity which scorned those same 'rules' altogether. His admiration is for the 'sounder few' whose common sense led them to a middle way, restoring (with a deliberate allusion to the Restoration of Charles II) the 'fundamental laws' of Nature which hold sway over the self-declared Augustan Age of English literature.

Pope's polished heroic couplets reveal much about the taste of the age and about his own aspirations as a poet, but he never has occasion to consider a particular author or text in detail; as a result, his advice is too generalised to be of any practical value, and perhaps too confident for its own good. He may mock Boileau for being over-rigid, but it is not at all clear that he avoids the same fault himself; unlike Dryden, he makes no allowance for the possibility that particular texts may need to be appreciated in ways that the ancients had never foreseen. Good taste, for Pope, is something which does not change down the years; it is always there, waiting to be identified and practised by the discerning few. Now that he and his contemporaries have rediscovered it, the implication seems to be that poetry and criticism have nowhere left to go.

Joseph Addison   1672–1719

Addison deserves a place in any history of literary criticism not because he made any significant contribution to critical theory or because he had the revealing insights of a major writer, but because he was the first to practise criticism in the form which is now most familiar to us. Sidney,

---

*Nicolas Boileau (1636–1711), a French poet and critic who advocated strict adherence to neoclassical principles.

Jonson, Dryden and Pope all write as if their readers are, at least potentially, fellow-authors, and so see criticism as the business of advising them how to write, as well as recommending or justifying certain kinds of writing, notably their own, over others. But Addison sets himself up as an intermediary between authors and their readers, who are no longer potential authors themselves but men of average taste and education who want guidance on what to read and what to look for in their reading. He is, in effect, the first reviewer – though not, as it happens, of contemporary works.

All Addison's most influential critical writing appeared in the first run of *The Spectator* (1711–12), the periodical which he and Richard Steele* introduced as a successor to *The Tatler*, offering essays mainly on manners, morals and literature. He contributed a number of essays on the topic of 'wit', laying the usual Augustan stress on the lively display of good sense rather than merely playing with words; similarly, his contributions 'on the pleasures of the imagination' are typically eighteenth-century in that they concentrate on the visual content and effect of literature, to the exclusion of much else. Most effective of all, however, were the eighteen weekly numbers, from January to May 1712, which Addison devoted to a detailed discussion of Milton's *Paradise Lost*.

He began with six issues on general topics concerning the poem, and followed with twelve more, each reviewing one of its books. He makes a bold bid to break out of the whole neoclassical obsession with 'rules' and definitions:

> There is nothing in Nature so irksome as general discourses, especially when they turn chiefly upon words. For this reason I shall waive the discussion of that point which was started some years since, whether Milton's *Paradise Lost* may be called an heroic poem? Those who will not give it that title, may call it (if they please) a Divine Poem. It will be sufficient to its perfection, if it has in it all the beauties of the highest kind of poetry; and as for those who say it is not an heroick poem, they advance no more to the diminution of it than if they should say Adam is not Aeneas, nor Eve Helen. (*Spectator*, No. 267)

It sounds refreshingly as if Addison is going to confront the poem as it stands, without bothering to debate the category or genre to which it belongs, but in fact most of his general discussion of the poem is conducted in terms of whether or not it measures up to the rules of the epic, such as having a plot with action which is one, entire and great. All his main objections to the poem concern its supposed indecorums as an epic: it has a hero, Adam, whose fortunes decline (more appropriate for

---

*Sir Richard Steele (1672–1729) was an Anglo-Irish playwright, journalist and political commentator.

tragedy, surely, though he tries to defend Milton on this by floating the possibility that Christ is the real hero of the poem); it has too many digressions; it has too many heathen references for a Christian epic, and so on. The papers on individual books are even more disappointing since, although they quote extensively from the text, they offer little real discussion or analysis. Addison declares that his job is 'to point out [the poem's] particular beauties, and to determine wherein they consist', which turns out in practice to mean that he acts as a kind of enthusiastic tour-guide, pointing out notable beauty-spots and labelling them as 'sublime' or 'natural' (rather in the manner of Longinus), but making no effort to explain how these effects are achieved or even to elucidate the obscurer parts of the text. Addison's essays on *Paradise Lost*, which were later collected in book form and remained popular throughout the century, amount to a literary Baedecker or Michelin Guide, making sure that the willing but uninformed reader did not miss what 'good taste' deemed to be noteworthy. Much criticism since then has been written in this vein, and has often proved as popular as Addison found it to be; but in failing to ask root questions about the value of literature and how it works, such criticism merely degenerates into being a simplified *substitute* for real literature (a kind of 'Milton Made Easy') and no real contribution to its understanding or appreciation.

The rise of the novel

The early eighteenth century saw the early development of the dominant literary form of modern times, the novel. But it is a development about which the formal literary criticism of the time has nothing whatever to say. Classical precedents had nothing to offer that was directly relevant to the new form, which was, partly for that reason, generally thought to be beneath the consideration of men of taste. As a result, the only significant critical statements came from those novelists who felt the need to explain and justify their own works. John Bunyan (1628–88), for example, prefaces his proto-novel, *The Pilgrim's Progress* (1678), with a verse 'Apology' in which he attempts to excuse his foray into allegorical fiction; as a Puritan of sorts he is especially conscious of the objection that all literature is a telling of untruths and a dangerous distraction from more serious matters. He tries to counter this with the fact that The Bible uses parables (quoting Hosea 12:10 'I have used similitudes', on the title-page), suggesting that even obscure fictions may be an indirect way to deeper truths:

> Why, what's the matter? 'It is dark.' What tho'?
> 'But it is feigned.' What of it, I trow?
> Some men by feigning words as dark as mine,
> Make truth to spangle, and its rays to shine.

'But they want solidness.' Speak man thy mind.
'They drowned the weak; metaphors make us blind.'
. . . must I needs want solidness, because
By metaphors I speak; was not God's laws,
His Gospel-laws in olden time held forth
By types, shadows and metaphors?

This is an odd twist to the conventional neoclassical habit of justifying works by reference and comparison to honoured precedents. Daniel Defoe (c.1660–1731) approaches a similar problem very differently in his preface to *Moll Flanders* (1722); he pretends throughout that his novel is a true story, as told by the supposed heroine, albeit 'put into new words, and the style . . . a little altered'. Defoe apparently believes that his fictions will be more credible, or at least acceptable, if the pretence that they are an authentic record of actual events is maintained. Against the objection that it is inherently a vicious and depraved story – perhaps because it is so true-to-life – he protests:

All possible care . . . has been taken to give no lewd ideas, no immodest turns in the new dressing up this story . . . . Throughout the infinite variety of this book, this fundamental is most strictly adhered to; there is not a wicked action in any part of it, but it is first or last rendered unhappy and unfortunate . . . there is not an ill thing mentioned but it is condemned, even in the relation, nor a virtuous, just thing but it carries its praise along with it . . . . Upon this foundation this book is recommended to the reader, as a work from every part of which something may be learned, and some just and religious inference is drawn, by which the reader will have something of instruction if he pleases to make use of it.

It may be objected that Defoe wishes to have his cake and eat it too: on the one hand he offers an authentic account of what we may expect to be a thoroughly depraved life and on the other he promises us pious instruction. Defoe is clearly (though perhaps not very seriously – his main point is to attract readers) trying to argue that a book may be virtuous even if it has inherently vicious subject-matter – that style and narrative technique may, so to speak, override content. At the same time he is worried that too open an admission of his own authorial guiding-hand will diminish the credibility of the first-person narration. Much later criticism of the novel returns to these questions raised but only imperfectly answered by Defoe: the moral purpose of the novel, its credibility as a depiction of reality, the complex role of the author/narrator in mediating between the subject-matter and the reader.

Of the early novelists only Henry Fielding (1707–54) made a serious and sustained attempt to justify the novel in *theoretical* terms, and no one was to follow his lead for over a century. In the preface to *Joseph Andrews* (1742), Fielding tried to extend traditional neoclassical theories of literature to include a new form, the 'comic epic-poem in prose'. It is not to be confused with stage comedy, inasmuch as 'its action [is] more extended and comprehensive; containing a much larger circle of incidents, and introducing a greater variety of characters.' The work is to be understood as a form of history or biography, since it deals principally with one central individual involved in a particular set of circumstances and a particular social context; on the other hand, Fielding never makes any serious pretence that his characters are actual people – they are only real in the sense that they depict types who are universally familiar: 'The lawyer is not only alive, but hath been so these 4000 years', as he puts it in Book III, Chapter 1. To justify the comic dimension to his 'epic-poem in prose', he suggests that it differs from earlier prose romances in its ludicrous diction, its disposition towards parody and its concentration on the affected and ridiculous aspects of human nature: that is, the prose epic is to the traditional verse epic as stage comedy is to stage tragedy (dealing with lower persons in a ludicrous way). He borrows from Ben Jonson's theory of 'humorous' characterisation to explain the kind of comedy he envisages: 'The only course of the true ridiculous is affectation' and 'affectation proceeds from one of these two causes: vanity or hypocrisy'. While it is true that much of the comedy in his two major novels, *Joseph Andrews* and *Tom Jones* (1749), does arise from the satirical exposure of such affectation (together with elements of mock-heroic parody and burlesque), it is also clear that many of the effects of both his own and other authors' novels simply cannot be explained within neoclassical terminology; his ideas of characterisation, for example, apply far more comfortably to drama than they do to the novel – never being able to take into account the prolonged time-span of reading and the peculiar relationship which inevitably grows up between a reader and the principal characters of a novel.

Fielding may have come to recognise that this sort of terminology was inadequate for dealing with the novel. In *Tom Jones* all eighteen books lead off with a critical preface; but after the first few they really have very little to say and degenerate into a kind of running joke in themselves: 'These soporific parts are so many scenes of Serious artfully interwoven, in order to contrast and set off the rest.' This may be a kind of double-bluff, of a sort that Fielding could well have learned from Ben Jonson: that the point of the critical material which he weaves into his novels is not so much to offer acute theoretical insights into what he writes as to keep reminding readers of an essential basic truth, that what he writes is fiction not fact, art not life. As such it must be judged in different ways and by different criteria from life itself. It was partly because, in

Fielding's view, Samuel Richardson* had fudged these distinctions in his novel *Pamela*, that he turned to fiction himself with *Shamela* (1741) and *Joseph Andrews*. (We have already seen the ambiguity that Defoe got himself into on these questions.) In the end it is Fielding's conviction that the novel is art, and therefore potentially 'Serious', that makes his forays into criticism valuable, even though the traditional vocabulary at his disposal is not able, for all his facetious adaptations, to express this adequately. The only other major author of the period to pursue the idea that the novel is art, in spite of a comprehensiveness which is easily mistaken for life, was Laurence Sterne† in *Tristram Shandy* (1760-7), but it would be difficult – not to say dangerous – to abstract a serious critical theory from that brilliant but whimsical novel.

Samuel Johnson   1709-1784

Dr Johnson stands as a great breakwater in English literary criticism, being the last major man of letters whose instinctive first question on any question was 'what would the ancients have said?' yet having the courage of very independent convictions which have made him a model for all subsequent critics. His achievement undoubtedly owes something to the time in which he lived, inasmuch as his two major critical works, the Preface to his edition of *The Plays of William Shakespeare* (1765) and his *Lives of the English Poets* (1779-81), appeared when England had acquired an established literary tradition, containing figures as unmistakably major as Spenser, Shakespeare, Milton, Dryden and Pope. This helped to give Johnson something which none of his English predecessors had possessed with any consistency, a historical perspective, an appreciation that taste and styles change and that some literary achievements cannot be accounted for by reference to the neoclassical 'rules'. On the other hand, Johnson was sufficiently an Augustan to believe that certain basic qualities are essential in literature, and that the job of the critic is primarily to assess the extent to which they are present in any particular piece. Add to these rather conflicting attributes two qualities peculiar to Johnson – an acute, almost over-acute, sensitivity to moral questions, to words themselves and to the morbid side of life; and a constitutional laziness which led to odd lapses of concentration – and we have the characteristic tone of his criticism: magisterial yet often in a liberal cause; authoritative yet sometimes idiosyncratically personal; sweepingly confident in his generalisations but sometimes omitting to pursue his insights with real intellectual curiosity.

---

*Richardson (1689-1761), a printer, was also a very effective novelist, author of *Pamela* (1741), *Clarissa* (1747-8) and *Sir Charles Grandison* (1753-4).
†Sterne (1713-68) was a clergyman and author of novels cast in a sentimental vein, such as *A Sentimental Journey* (1768).

Johnson's consideration of Shakespeare begins with the observation that it is one hundred and fifty years since his death: 'The Poet ... may now begin to assume the dignity of an ancient, and claim the privilege of established fame and prescriptive veneration.' As with the Greek and Roman classics, length of survival and continued approbation amount to a *prima facie* case for greatness. Johnson sometimes flirts with the idea that a democratic consensus – what pleases most people most of the time – might establish classic status in literature: it appeals to the robust common sense of his nature. But he is too aware of the fickleness of taste finally to allow this: 'approbation, though long continued, may yet be only the approbation of prejudice or fashion'. He needs more certain criteria by which to establish Shakespeare's greatness.

'Nothing can please many, and please long, but just representations of general nature . . . . Shakespeare is above all writers, at least above all modern writers, the poet of nature; the poet that holds up to his readers a faithful mirror of manners and life.' This is the true Augustan in Johnson and the key to what he approves – and disapproves – of in Shakespeare. So, he approves of the fact that, whereas 'in the writings of other poets a character is too often an individual; in those of Shakespeare it is commonly a species.' Shakespeare's 'mirror' is most faithful, in Johnson's view, when it eschews the particular, the odd or the quirky in favour of general truths – and he finds this most often in the comedies, which he judges to be 'instinct' on Shakespeare's part, rather than in the tragedies which use 'skill'. To a later age, both preferences – general truths and comedies – may seem misguided, but it is these which lead Johnson to a liberating defence of Shakespeare's 'mixed' style of drama:

> Shakespeare's plays are not in the rigorous and critical sense either tragedies or comedies, but compositions of a distinct kind; exhibiting the real state of sublunary nature, which partakes of good and evil, joy and sorrow . . . . That this is a practice contrary to the rules of criticism will be readily allowed; but there is always an appeal open from criticism to nature.

Criticism was only valid, in Pope's terms, inasmuch as it was 'Nature methodiz'd'; if literature breaks the rules of criticism but not of nature, it may still lay claim to greatness and this is the essence of Johnson's case for Shakespeare.

But, using the same criterion, Johnson can find much to blame as well as to praise. Without ever saying it baldly, he implies that a true mirroring of nature will always reveal a moral pattern, and this is frequently lacking in Shakespeare:

> He sacrifices virtue to convenience, and is so much more careful to please than to instruct, that he seems to write without any moral

purpose. From his writings indeed a system of social duty may be selected, for he that thinks reasonably must think morally; but his precepts and axioms drop casually from him; he makes no just distribution of good or evil.

He also argues that Shakespeare's plays are often badly constructed and not as careful or as decorous in their language as they might be. He concludes that Shakespeare's most characteristic fault is a delight in quibbles:

> A quibble is to Shakespeare what luminous vapours are to the traveller; he follows it at all adventures; it is sure to lead him out of his way, and sure to engulf him in the mire . . . a quibble was to him the fatal Cleopatra for which he lost the world, and was content to lose it.

In this strangely impassioned passage Johnson seems to let loose all his pent-up frustration that Shakespeare, the 'poet of nature', should waste so much of his talent on irrelevant details of language, character, plot or whatever, rather than concentrating on the general truth which he is so uniquely qualified to depict.

Having thus weighed Shakespeare's claim to greatness as 'the poet of nature', finding evidence both for and against, Johnson clinches the case by considering what many might consider his most flagrant vice – his non-observance of the supposed Aristotelian 'unities'. He sets out – 'not dogmatically, but deliberately' – to demolish the authority of the 'unities' by Shakespeare's example; Johnson does not intend to subvert *all* earlier critical precepts, but to reinforce the idea that nature rather than criticism is the final arbiter, and thereby to establish Shakespeare as a kind of latter-day Homer: that is, the kind of writer who 'defines' nature for lesser mortals and is not confined by their inadequate prescriptions. He has already disposed of the unity of action in asserting that a mixture of tragedy and comedy exhibits 'the real state of sublunary nature'. 'The necessity of observing the unities of time and place arises from the supposed necessity of making the drama credible' – some people think that audiences will only 'credit' drama if it approximates as closely as possible to the circumstances of reality. But this completely overlooks the faculty of imagination:

> The truth is, that the spectators are always in their senses, and know, from the first act to the last, that the stage is only a stage, and that the players are only players . . . where is the absurdity of allowing that space to represent first Athens, and then Sicily, which was always known to be neither Sicily nor Athens, but a modern theatre? . . . . Time is, of all modes of existence, most obsequious to the imagination; a lapse of years is as easily conceived as a passage of hours.

Johnson was not the first to voice doubts about the 'unities', but he was the first to confront them with such overwhelming common sense. They are never a serious issue in English literary criticism again, but Shakespeare – by whose example Johnson defies them – becomes its central abiding concern. The Shakespeare we enjoy today is not the Shakespeare Johnson enjoyed, nor can we always agree with even the latter's smallest assertions (for example his remark that 'A play read, affects the mind like a play acted'); but Johnson was the last critic really able to hold Shakespeare at arm's length – to balance what he saw as negative qualities against immensely impressive positive ones. To later generations Shakespeare has become virtually untouchable, a model of · literary perfection – though it is not always clear what criteria critics are using when they hold it to be so. Johnson's Preface, with its degree of scepticism, with its conviction that – however great his talent was – Shakespeare was only human, remains required reading both in the history of literary criticism and in our appreciation of England's greatest author.

Johnson's *Lives of the English Poets* has been hardly less influential than his Preface; it established biographical criticism – the consideration of literature in context of its author's life and career – as the most widely-read form of criticism in English. For all the critical 'movements' that have emerged since, this is probably still the case. Johnson did not invent biographical criticism, or even the specific form that it took in these essays – where he offers firstly a biography, then a 'character' of the poet and finally an appreciation of his works – but he performed the task so memorably and monumentally here, bringing to it all the learning and authority that went into his *Dictionary*, that he must be credited with imposing this approach as the nearest thing there has been to a successor to the neoclassical 'rules'. No modern student will instinctively ask whether an author has followed the advice of Aristotle or Horace, but most will ask when he lived, what his preoccupations were, where a work belongs in his career, how it compares with earlier and later works – all questions of biographical criticism.

The range of the *Lives* is extensive, covering most of the poets, major and minor, of the previous one hundred and twenty years. This tends to obscure the fact that Johnson does not offer – indeed, scarcely purports to offer – objective accounts of these authors. Even leaving aside the 'Life of Richard Savage' – written much earlier than the other Lives and essentially a tribute to a personal friend – there is an unmistakable strain of special pleading in Johnson's criticism. He is primarily concerned to justify the Augustan mode of poetry, of which he himself had been one of the last exponents and which was all but defunct by the time he wrote these essays – more than thirty years after the death of Pope. So the early Lives, such as that of Cowley, give a memorable account of what existed before the Augustans, notably the 'Metaphysical' style. (Johnson's comments on this are quoted more extensively in the next chapter, in relation to Donne's *Songs and Sonets*.) It is clear that Johnson understood 'Metaphysical' poetry, and could describe it well, with occasional grudging admiration, such as 'To write on their plan, it was at least necessary to read and think'; but also that he could not approve of what he saw as their over-ingenious originality: 'they broke every image into fragments; and could no more represent . . . the prospect of nature, or the scenes of life, than he who dissects a sunbeam with a prism can exhibit the wide effulgence of a summer noon.' They had not, in short, discovered the Augustan truth that 'great thoughts are always general.' In the later Lives, Johnson is even more harsh on recent writers such as Gray, who have seen what Augustanism is capable of but who have abandoned it in favour of new styles and versification which were eventually to produce Romantic poetry; only the 'Elegy, Written in a Country Churchyard', which, Johnson says, 'abounds with images which find a mirror in every mind, and with sentiments to which every bosom returns an echo' – the Augustan ideal – escapes a general carping on Gray's florid language and outlandish verse-forms.

At the heart of the *Lives* lie two great essays, on the poets who approach closest to Johnson's ideal, Dryden and Pope, and also one on the unmistakably major figure of the period who does not – Milton. On the whole, Johnson writes his Lives as if the three parts – biography, character and works – have no necessary connection with each other; he does not imply that a poet's life or character *explains* or *justifies* what he writes. But with Milton in particular he seems to deviate somewhat from this principle and allow his antipathy to Milton's political and religious ideas to colour his estimate of the man's works: 'His political notions were those of an acrimonious and surly republican . . . founded in an envious hatred of greatness, and a sullen desire of independence; in petulance impatient of control, and pride disdainful of superiority.' While constantly deferring to Milton's classic status as an author, he never loses an opportunity to point out what seem to him deficiencies in particular works. Of *Lycidas* (1645), for example: 'the diction is harsh, the rhymes uncertain, and the numbers unpleasing . . . . Where there is leisure for fiction there is little grief . . . . Its form is that of a pastoral, easy, vulgar, and therefore disgusting.' Of *Paradise Lost*:

> The plan . . . has this inconvenience, that it comprises neither human actions nor human manners. The man and woman who act and suffer are in a state which no other man or woman can ever know. The reader . . . has therefore little natural curiosity or sympathy . . . . The want of human interest is always felt. *Paradise Lost* is one of the books which the reader admires and lays down, and forgets to take up again. None ever wished it longer than it is.

In short, it is not an Augustan poem; Johnson is aware that it has qualities of greatness which do not fall within his own definitions of what matters in poetry but, rather than explore these, he seems to be determined to cut this 'surly republican' down to size.

Such criticism – a calculated attack on a major author – can be exhilarating to read; but it is a dangerous example to imitate. The lesson to derive from Johnson's comments on Milton is that Milton *mattered* to Johnson, both as a thinker and as a poet, and this is why his criticism is so engaged, albeit so negative. Johnson is measuring his own standards and principles against those of a man he respects but with whom he is not in sympathy; such criticism is not to be undertaken lightly. He is generally a better model when assessing Dryden and Pope, two poets who in different ways come closest to his ideal; the comparison of the two, in the *Life of Pope*, is particularly illuminating and suggestive:

> Dryden knew more of man in his general nature, and Pope in his local manners. The notions of Dryden were formed by comprehensive speculation, and those of Pope by minute attention . . . . It is not to be inferred of this poetical vigour Pope had only a little, because Dryden had more; for every other writer since Milton must give place to Pope; and even of Dryden it must be said, that, if he has brighter paragraphs, he has not better poems . . . . If the flights of Dryden are therefore higher, Pope continues longer on the wing. If of Dryden's fire the blaze is brighter, of Pope's the heat is more regular and constant. Dryden often surpasses expectation, and Pope never falls below it. Dryden is read with frequent astonishment, and Pope with perpetual delight.

The acute powers of discrimination demonstrated here, between two poets who – to a superficial modern reading – often seem very similar, cannot be ignored, though of course we are by no means obliged to subscribe to the value-judgements which go with them.

Although Johnson's *Lives of the English Poets* may be said to have established literary biography as the most popular medium of criticism in England, they cannot be said to have established a model form which others were to follow. Later writers were to blur the distinctions between biography, character and appreciation of the works in a variety of ways, producing results which are only marginally related to the concerns of literary criticism as we have defined them. In the case of some writers – notably those who died young and dramatically, like Marlowe, Keats, Byron and some First World War poets – the biographical approach can prove particularly suspect, colouring the whole process of understanding and appreciating what they actually wrote.

The fact is that there are myriad ways in which the life and times of an author can be brought to bear on an understanding of his writing – so many that it has proved impossible to establish an orthodoxy on how it should or should not be done. The two most influential theorists on this question were both French: **Charles Augustin Sainte-Beuve** (1804–69) and **Hippolyte Adolphe Taine** (1828–93).

Sainte-Beuve advocated a style of literary biography in which the critic establishes as nearly as possible a sympathetic identification with his subject, in order to bring the man and his writing to life:

> To get inside one's author, to establish oneself there, to exhibit him from all points of view; to make him live, move and speak as he must have done, to follow him as far as possible into his inner life and private manners; to tie him on all sides to this earth, this real existence, these daily habits which are as much a part of great men as the rest of us.

This approach is heavily influenced by the Romantic conception of the author as a great and specially gifted man, the greatness of whose works is almost indistinguishable from the special qualities of his vision and talent.

Taine, by contrast, saw the study of literature as an adjunct of moral and social history; using the methods of observation of a biologist, a critic might enquire into the life and works of an author not merely for information about that individual but in order to discern certain fundamental laws or principles of man's moral and social being:

> a literary work is not a mere individual play of imagination, the isolated caprice of an excited brain, but a transcript of contemporary manners, a manifestation of a certain kind of mind . . . we might discover, from the monuments of literature, a knowledge of the manner in which men thought and felt centuries ago.

Taine is the father of the sociology of literature, advocating the study of authors and texts in a quasi-scientific manner for the light they may throw on man as a social being. His equation of literary biography with the methods of biology is symptomatic of mid-nineteenth-century preoccupations. Like all other forms of literary criticism, the precise focus and application of literary biography have moved with the times.

William Wordsworth 1770–1850

Wordsworth's Preface to *Lyrical Ballads* (first included in the second edition of 1800; revised with an Appendix, 1802) is one of the revolutionary works of criticism, helping to usher in the Romantic Age in literature. But it is also in many ways a confused and unsatisfactory essay because Wordsworth frequently has difficulty knowing what to make of his own radically new ideas. He is primarily concerned to justify the kinds of poems which he had contributed to *Lyrical Ballads* (first edition, 1798); Coleridge had also contributed to the volume (notably 'The Ancient Mariner'), but Wordsworth does not concern himself with his friend's works. His poems were radically unlike anything produced by the neoclassical and Augustan poets championed by Johnson; they included stories of simple country folk and rustic ballads:

> The principal object . . . proposed in these poems was to choose incidents and situations from common life, and to relate or describe them, throughout, as far as was possible in a selection of language really used by men, and, at the same time, to throw over them a certain colouring of imagination, whereby ordinary things should be presented to the mind in an unusual aspect; and, further, and above all, to make these incidents and situations interesting by tracing in them, truly though not ostentatiously, the primary laws of our nature . . . . Humble and rustic life was generally chosen, because, in that condition, the essential passions of the heart find a better soil in which they can attain their maturity . . . . The language, too, of these men has been adopted (purified indeed from what appear to be its real defects, from all lasting and rational causes of dislike or disgust) because such men hourly communicate with the best objects from which the best part of language is originally derived.

An earlier critic would have found nothing objectionable in Wordsworth's declared aim of 'tracing . . . the primary laws of our nature'. It is the ways in which he sought to do it that are new: concentrating on 'common' and 'rustic life' in the proper language of such situations and throwing over it 'a certain colouring of imagination'. All this is far removed from the polite conversation of gentlemen on man's role as a social being, which is the starting-point of a Dryden, Pope or Johnson in the quest for 'the primary laws of our nature'.

Wordsworth is recommending not only a new style of poetry but a whole new definition of what poetry – and poets – should be:

> Let me ask, what is meant by the word Poet? What is a Poet? To whom does he address himself? . . . . He is a man speaking to men: a man, it is true, endowed with more lively sensibility, more enthusiasm and tenderness, who has a greater knowledge of human nature, and a more comprehensive soul, than are supposed to be common among mankind.

To the neoclassical critic the poet had been a craftsman – a gifted one, no doubt, but essentially a man like any other, observing and reproducing general nature with the help of ancient precedent and the 'rules'. To Wordsworth, the poet, despite some half-hearted protestations to the contrary, is a man apart, with a special sensibility and enthusiasm. Enthusiasm is no longer a term of abuse but one of praise. The poet purveys a special insight into the human condition: 'The Poet writes under one restriction only, namely, the necessity of giving immediate pleasure to a human being possessed of that information which may be expected from him, not as a lawyer, a physician, a mariner, an astronomer, or a natural philosopher, but as a Man.' Here again there is nothing that would immediately be objectionable to Pope or Johnson; the difference is that 'Man', for Wordsworth, is the newly ennobled creature described by Rousseau,* with the liberated spirit of the American and French Revolutions; hence Wordsworth's determination to study Man in the most natural circumstances possible. He is anxious also to write in the language of men, stripped admittedly of its vulgarities but falling into neither artificial poetic diction nor the jargon of lawyers, doctors or similar specialists. Hence Wordsworth's egalitarian wish to believe that his poet is a man like any other, but it is clear that anyone able to 'trace the primary laws of our nature' as he intends must have special gifts: 'the Poet is chiefly distinguished from other men by a greater promptness to think and feel without immediate external excitement, and a greater power in expressing such thoughts and feelings as are produced in him in that manner.' Nevertheless, he insists 'these passions and thoughts and feelings are the general passions and thoughts and feelings of men.'

Where Wordsworth reveals his true Romantic colours, and begins – for all his protestations – to make the poet a man apart, is in his attempt to describe the creative process, making that the key to authentic poetry:

> poetry is the spontaneous overflow of powerful feelings: it takes its origin from emotion recollected in tranquillity: the emotion is contemplated till, by a species of re-action, the tranquillity gradually disappears, and an emotion, kindred to that which before was the subject of contemplation, is gradually produced, and does itself actually exist in the mind. In this mood successful composition generally begins . . .

Virtually all earlier criticism starts from the ancient Greek assumption that art is a *mimetic* activity, imitating, copying or mirroring nature in some form; in discussing the creative process in this way Wordsworth begins to suggest that poetry may derive not so much from imitating nature as from *imaginatively re-creating it*. (Notice the earlier suggestion about throwing 'a certain colouring of imagination' over 'incidents and situations from common life'.) The poet himself, with his special sensitivity and powers of imagination, becomes the focus of attention.

*Jean-Jacques Rousseau (1712–78), French-Swiss moralist and philosopher, was the author of *La Nouvelle Héloise* (1751) and *The Social Contract* (1752).

The chief problem with Wordsworth's definitions of poetry and his description of how it operates is that they leave out two essential factors. The first is what we might call the craft of poetry: how does the 'spontaneous overflow of powerful feelings' actually find a form of words? The second is a recognition that the form of words which is found is ultimately different from, and independent of, both the emotions from which it derived and those it may create in a reader. Wordsworth seems to imply that if the poet *feels* deeply enough, the right words will somehow come – a sentiment which has inspired some very immature and self-indulgent poetry – and that they will be capable of inspiring similar feelings in a reader. These weaknesses are most apparent when he tries to explain why he, or any other poet, writes in verse which, after all, seems a long way removed from the natural language he had earlier advocated: he starts by suggesting that metre limits the intensity of emotion, preventing it from becoming too painful or powerful (though later in the same essay he suggests that metre actually intensifies emotion) and ends lamely by asking: 'Why should I be condemned for attempting to superadd to such description the charm which, by the consent of all nations, is acknowledged to exist in metrical language?' In laying such stress on the naturalness of poetry, concentrating on its emotional force and content – rejecting the old mechanical rules and the artificial language of much neoclassical poetry – Wordsworth has not come up with any convincing argument for why he writes in verse at all.

For all its confusion and special pleading, Wordsworth's Preface to *Lyrical Ballads* marks a crucial turning-point in the way critics look at poetry. There is more than a touch of puritan self-conviction about his thinking: the poet is sufficiently different from other men in his deep sensitivity and powers of expression as to be a law unto himself; no one can lay down laws as to how he must write. Although he is 'a man speaking to men', his poetry is forged by a specially gifted consciousness. Here are the seeds of one of the great modern myths: poets as men apart, subject only to self-imposed constraints, outsiders both mentally and socially, Shelley's 'unacknowledged legislators of the world' (in *A Defence of Poetry*, 1821, published 1840).

Samuel Taylor Coleridge   1772–1834

Of all English critics, it is most difficult to do justice to Coleridge. He was primarily concerned with the aesthetics and psychology of literary creation; how original he was in this and how much he appropriated from German writers such as Schlegel* are still unresolved questions.

---

*Friederich von Schlegel (1772–1829) was a German writer and critic whose works inspired the early German Romantic movement.

All his criticisms of particular texts and authors are related to these abstruse concerns in ways which it is difficult to summarise briefly. There is an additional problem, in that much of his critical thinking has come down to us in unsatisfactory – often second-hand – versions; even his most sustained critical work, *Biographia Literaria* (1817) was written very hastily and on idiosyncratic principles.

Coleridge's most influential passages of criticism occur in those chapters of *Biographia Literaria* (14, 17–20, 22) in which he considers Wordsworth's poetry and points out a number of deficiencies in the Preface to *Lyrical Ballads*. What is so special, he asks, about the language of rustics once it has been 'purified' of its rusticity? Does not Wordsworth's own poetry demonstrate that there are more significant linguistic differences between verse and prose than he will admit? 'Were there excluded from Mr. Wordsworth's poetic composition all that a literal adherence to the theory of his Preface would exclude, two thirds at least of the marked beauties of his poetry must be erased.' But these observations are subsidiary to a more fundamental consideration that Coleridge feels compelled to make of what constitutes poetry and a poet:

> A poem is that species of composition, which is opposed to works of science, by proposing for its immediate object pleasure, not truth; and from all other species (having this object in common with it), it is discriminated by proposing to itself such delight from the whole, as is compatible with a distinct gratification from each component part.

This is the most succinct statement of the theory of the organic unity of poetry/literature: a poem is to be judged not as a mirror of truth – as we judge science – but as a thing in itself, almost as a living organism, which cannot be measured by extrinsic standards, but only by its own internal consistency: 'nothing can permanently please, which does not contain in itself the reason why it is so, and not otherwise.' This is why Coleridge will have nothing to do with metre as a 'superadded' charm to poetry: it must be intrinsically necessary to the poem as a whole.

The organic unity of a poem is not something which can be imposed by adherence to mechanical rules but must derive from the poet's Imagination – a supremely vital gift of the few and which Coleridge distinguishes from the lesser, more mundane faculty of Fancy:

> The poet, described in *ideal* perfection, brings the whole soul of man into activity, with the subordination of its faculties to each other, according to their relative worth and dignity. He diffuses a tone and spirit of unity, that blends, and (as it were) *fuses*, each into each, by that synthetic and magical power, to which we have exclusively appropriated the name of imagination. This power, first put in action by the will and understanding, and retained under their irremissive, though gentle and unnoticed, control . . . reveals itself in the balance

or reconciliation of opposite or discordant qualities: of sameness, with difference; of the general, with the concrete; the idea, with the image; the individual, with the representative; the sense of novelty and freshness, with old and familiar objects; a more than usual state of emotion, with more than usual order; judgement ever-awake and steady self-possession, with enthusiasm and feeling profound or vehement; and while it blends and harmonizes the natural and the artificial, still subordinates art to nature; the manner to the matter; and our admiration of the poet to our sympathy with the poetry.

The implications of this concentrated passage are profound: such poets, it is clear, are born and not made; such poems may be judged only according to their own lights and not according to any established precept or precedent; their quality is in a very direct sense derived from the quality of the mind of their creator. This gave Coleridge a freedom in respect of assessing both modern and Elizabethan poets (particularly Shakespeare) which no previous critic had enjoyed: their works were not to be judged by extrinsically defined or artificially imposed standards, but in terms of their imaginative coherence.*

The principal omission in Coleridge's thesis is what we might call a social dimension: the poet he envisages is under no obligation to teach or to be useful in other ways; it is not even clear that his poetry will attempt to trace, in Wordsworth's terms, 'the primary laws of our nature'; there are, in fact, no restrictions on either his subject-matter or his style, beyond the requirement to give 'pleasure' – and this 'pleasure' will derive less from specifically accountable features than from the organic unity of the whole; this being so, the poet has no responsibilities to his reader or to anyone else – only to the poem. It is clear that Coleridge himself envisaged the poet as a man of great integrity as well as of special gifts, producing poems which would offer profound insights into man's imaginative, psychological, and, ultimately, moral being. But that is not explicitly required by the definitions which he expounds: the door is open for a poetry which is, to all intents and purposes, about itself and for itself, art for art's sake, Romantic self-indulgence. But the narrow-minded features of neoclassicism and of literature seen simplistically as a 'mirror' of reality died with Coleridge, apparently forever.

Matthew Arnold   1822–1888

The eminence of the great critical manifestos of the Romantic poets – not only those of Wordsworth and Coleridge, but Keats's letters

*It is no accident that Coleridge's critical reputation has been at its highest with I. A. Richards (1893–1981) and many of the New Critics in the first half of this century: his insistence on the poem as a self-contained, self-defining, self-justifying organism fits well with the kind of 'practical criticism' which they advocate. See pp. 68–72 below.

56 · An outline history of literary criticism

and Shelley's *A Defence of Poetry* – obscures the fact that the bread-and-butter criticism of the nineteenth century was conducted on very different principles. Periodicals such as Blackwood's *Edinburgh Magazine* and *The Quarterly Review*, successors to Addison's *Spectator*, were widely read and influential; these two, for example, delivered famously crushing reviews of Keats's *Endymion*, which some people later condemned for their effect on the poet's health. On the whole such periodicals, like their modern successors, tended to be partisan in the opinions they disseminated, favouring certain 'schools' of literature as much as they favoured political parties; the appreciation of literature went side by side with an interest in other areas of knowledge – scientific, political, artistic, social – all of which might be projected with a certain 'colouring'. So, for example, the *Edinburgh Review* had Whig sympathies and was relatively progressive (though it had no time initially for Wordsworth and the 'Lake Poets'), while the *Quarterly Review* had a Tory bias and tended to be conservative.

Matthew Arnold's criticism needs to be seen against this background, and against the great social and theological debates of Victorian England, since it is clear that his thoughts on literature are of a piece with his equally distinguished thinking on those topics in works such as *Culture and Anarchy* and *Literature and Dogma*. *Essays in Criticism, First Series* (1865) is a direct attack on what Arnold sees as the narrowness and provincialism of English thinking generally, and of English literary criticism in particular. Authors considered include Heine, Spinoza and Marcus Aurelius,* while there are also essays on such topics as 'The Literary Influence of Academies' and 'Pagan and Mediaeval Religious Sentiment.' No specifically English author or topic is discussed – a deliberate affront to the complacent belief that English culture, whether viewed through Whig *or* Tory spectacles, is perfect and self-sufficient in itself. Arnold wants a return to what he saw as the virtues of classical Greek civilisation: 'They regarded the whole: we regard the parts.' This volume contained nothing that we could describe as descriptive criticism, but it is prefaced by a theoretical essay on 'The Function of Criticism at the Present Time'. In this he declares himself to be 'bound by my own definition of criticism: *a disinterested endeavour to learn and propagate the best that is known and thought in the world.*' 'Disinterested' here does not imply that Arnold is only interested in literature in and for itself; on the contrary, he is convinced that literature can be a spiritually liberating and redeeming force in the world, on a par, at the least, with religion. What it does imply is that, since literature is potentially so

*Heinrich Heine (1797–1856) was a major German lyric and satiric poet; Benedictus de Spinoza (1632–77) an influential Dutch metaphysical philosopher; and Marcus Aurelius (AD 121–180) a Roman emperor (161–180), the author of *Meditations*, reflections on stoicism.

important, criticism of it must not be allowed to sink into mere prejudice or partisanship, narrow-mindedness of any kind. Recent English literature, as well as criticism, has, he believes, a narrowness which is not true of continental literature – in which Goethe* stands as his model of the ideal author:

> Byron's poetry had so little endurance in it, and Goethe's so much; both Byron and Goethe had a great productive power, but Goethe's was nourished by a great critical effort providing the true materials for it, and Byron's was not; Goethe knew life and the world, the poet's necessary subjects, much more comprehensively and thoroughly than Byron. He knew a great deal more of them, and he knew them more as they really are.

The attack is not aimed only at Byron, as Arnold makes clear in *Essays in Criticism, Second Series* (1888), largely made up of essays on the Romantic poets. Although he shows a good deal of enthusiasm for individual works and for the *potential* of Keats, Byron, Wordsworth and Shelley, in each he finds something lacking which disqualifies them as poets of the first order. In the prefatory essay to this volume, 'The Study of Poetry', he spells out his criteria: 'Neither the historical or the personal approach will aid us. Both approaches are fallacious since both are liable to make us praise or dispraise for reasons that have nothing to do with poetry.' We must be 'disinterested' – above merely historical or subjective considerations – if we are to identify and define the highest qualities in literature. He proposes a method similar to that suggested by Longinus to help us in this task: 'there can be no more useful help for discerning what poetry belongs to the class of the truly excellent, and can do us most good, than to have always in mind lines and expressions of the great masters, and to apply them as a touchstone to other poetry.' He offers examples of such 'touchstones' from Homer, Dante, Shakespeare and Milton – all of which, he believes, possess 'in the eminent degree, truth and seriousness', the hallmarks, for Arnold, of true excellence. He goes on to deny Chaucer and Burns the rank of classic status because they do not measure up to these standards; the latter is firmly disapproved of for his 'Scotch drink, Scotch religion, and Scotch manners'. The implication in the later essays is that all the English Romantic poets, in the last analysis, are unable to measure up to these taxing 'disinterested' standards.

The problem with Arnold is that, for all his insistence on being 'disinterested', he himself is nothing of the sort. Why should we accept *his* 'touchstones' of true excellence any more, for example, than we should accept those proposed by Longinus so many centuries before?

*Johann Wolfgang von Goethe (1749–1832), greatest of all German writers, was most famous for his *Faust* (1808, 1832).

Why should 'truth and seriousness' be *our* final criteria? He has elevated his own tastes, founded largely on the Greek classics, and his own morality to the level of absolutes without any real justification. As a result, he makes some of the most extravagant claims for literature ever made, such as 'The future of poetry is immense, because in poetry where it is worthy of its high destinies, our race, as time goes on, will find an ever surer and surer stay'. He is not, however, very helpful as a guide to understanding its variety and complexity. Perhaps Arnold's earnest insistence that the best poetry is extremely rare but that it can be morally beneficial, can be virtually a substitute for religion, 'can do us most good', is his most significant legacy, influencing later critics such as T. S. Eliot (1808–1965; see below, pp. 66–8) and F. R. Leavis.

Modern criticism

As we approach the twentieth century, it becomes increasingly difficult to write a historical outline of literary criticism as an account of individual contributions. The spread of education in general, and the adoption of literary criticism as a university subject in particular, has led to a great increase in critical activity and a marked diversity of approaches, so that it becomes almost invidious to single out individuals. The American novelist and critic Henry James's* contribution to the appreciation of the novel and T. S. Eliot's remarkably influential essays call for special attention, but for the rest broad approaches will be adopted, particular critics being cited as in some way representative of those approaches.

All three of the nineteenth century's most radically influential thinkers – Darwin, Marx and Freud† – have contributed to critical theory either directly or indirectly. **Charles Darwin** was not the first man to postulate a theory of evolution, but his *On the Origin of Species* (1859) offered the first substantial scientific 'proof' of such a theory, based on the principle of natural selection. The shock that this generated was profound. Earlier theories of evolution tended to be utopian in emphasis and could be squared relatively easily with ideas of a benign Divinity leading men to a higher destiny. Natural selection removed God from the picture altogether, making the rise and fall of species – man included – a matter of amoral, impersonal forces. Darwinianism thus became a burning issue in literature, particularly in the novel – for

*James (1843–1916) became a British citizen at the outbreak of the First World War and was awarded the Order of Merit in the year of his death.
†Charles Darwin (1809–82), the English naturalist who propounded the theory of organic evolution; Karl Marx (1818–83), German philosopher of history and the most influential figure in socialist thinking; Sigmund Freud (1856–1939), Austrian founder of psychoanalysis.

example, in the novels of Thomas Hardy and Samuel Butler's* *The Way of All Flesh* – and works were judged in the periodicals as being either pro- or anti-Darwin. Certain styles of writing came to be associated with Darwinian theories and the agnostic or atheistic doctrines which were assumed to follow from them; most notable among these was 'naturalism', the term adopted by the French novelist, Emile Zola (1840–1902). 'Naturalism' grew out of the earlier term, 'realism', a term originally associated with novelists such as Honoré de Balzac (1799–1850) who wanted to demonstrate that the novel was not simply escapist fantasy but a genuine (and useful) branch of literature, uniquely capable of recording man's social life in minute and particular detail. 'Naturalism' went further, implying that man's character was wholly *determined*, in a Darwinian way, by heredity and social environment; the 'naturalistic' novelist was determined to depict this with all the precision and inclusive detail of the biological scientist (and often with what the Victorians regarded as an unacceptable degree of frankness about man's alimentary and sexual functions).

(*The cases of 'realism' and 'naturalism' raise a general point about modern critical terminology, which it will be as well to clarify here. In the first instance they were purely descriptive terms, ways of trying to distinguish between one style of writing and another. But eventually they were adopted as labels, ways of identifying not only the style of a text but also its content, the author's outlook or philosophy, even his political sympathies. This is true of the vast majority of 'isms' which have been advanced to describe types of literature in the past century – 'Imagism', 'Symbolism', 'Modernism', for example. A critic therefore needs to be on his guard when he uses such terms, in case he implies more than he intends. A Dictionary of Critical Terms can be useful here.*)

In terms of literary theory, Darwin's ideas revived interest (by analogy, as it were) in the classical notion of literary 'species', that is of literary genres, each with its own characteristics and self-defining 'rules'. Throughout literary history there had been four main identifiable genres – dramatic, heroic, satiric and lyric – but criticism had largely confined itself to using them in a prescriptive fashion, trying to lay down laws about what an author could or could not do in any one of them, and occasionally worrying over which genre was the highest or most prestigious. Such considerations had been swept aside by the Romantics, who would not brook discussion of creativity in such mechanical or hierarchical terms. But the concept of genre was revived towards the end of the nineteenth century in a quasi-scientific spirit, as a useful way of describing and categorising possible varieties of literature

*Thomas Hardy (1840–1928), English novelist and poet, was the author of *The Mayor of Casterbridge* (1886), *Tess of the D'Urbervilles* (1891) and *Jude the Obscure* (1896). Samuel Butler (1835–1902) was an English satirist, novelist and critic.

(including completely new genres like the novel). The French critic, Ferdinand Brunetière (1849–1906) even attempted to discuss literary genres as if they behaved like biological species, being born, developing and eventually dying according to some inexorable laws analogous to those posited by Darwin. His book was called *The Evolution of Genres in the History of Literature* (1890). Ironically, Brunetière was using Darwinian terminology to prove exactly the opposite of what the proponents of 'naturalism' believed; he wanted to establish that literature was something self-contained, a valuable thing-in-itself, and not just a branch of sociology or social biology, as *avant-garde* novelists like Zola seemed to be suggesting. This demonstrates that the same *guru* can often plausibly be appropriated by opposed thinkers – in literary criticism as in so many areas of dispute. Less contentiously, genre-theory is still very much with us, a regular starting-point for much of the teaching of literature; one of its chief appeals is that it cuts across the view of literature as being the work of a particular author, or the product of a particular age or social environment (even cutting across language barriers). It may thus be useful in helping us to define what is specifically 'literary' about a text, what are the universal characteristics of literature. That is not to say, of course, that genre-theory is any more objective than any other approach to literature; it is by no means self-evident that any 'universal characteristics' exist in literature, or that they really matter if they do. Perhaps the most significant recent contribution to this field of enquiry is the Canadian critic Northrop Frye's (*b*.1912) *Anatomy of Criticism* (1957).

If Darwin has been adduced to bolster arguments of which it is doubtful if he would approve, how much more true is this of **Karl Marx**. Literature was not one of Marx's principal concerns, though he discusses it occasionally in his works on social and economic matters; like most European thinkers of the mid-nineteenth century, he was interested in it mainly as an adjunct to his interest in history. Works of literature, he insists, are as much a product of the social and economic conditions in which they were created as any other artefact:

> It is well known that Greek mythology constituted not only the arsenal of Greek art, but even the soil from which it grew. Is it possible that the attitude to nature and social relationships that lies at the heart of Greek fantasy, and therefore also of Greek art, could have existed in the presence of 'self-acting mules', railways, locomotives, and the electric telegraph? What could Vulcan do against Roberts and Co., Jupiter against the lightning rod . . . . Every mythology overcomes, subjugates and shapes the forces of nature in imagination and with its help. It disappears, consequently, with the actual mastery of these forces in nature (*Critique of Political Economy*, 1859).

By the same token, he argues, the kind of literature written by, for example, Shakespeare in the sixteenth century is a product of the prevailing social system of the time and of the economic realities which kept it in force.

Marx was sophisticated enough to recognise, however, that there is no simple equation between the *quality* of literary work and the social/economic development of the civilisation that produced it:

> With reference to art, it is known that the fixed periods of its greatest development do not correspond with the general development of society, nor, consequently, with the development of the material basis of the latter, which constitutes (so to speak) the skeleton of its organisation. For example, compare the Greeks and Shakespeare too with their contemporaries.

The *quality* of Greek art is somehow independent of its being produced by a slave-owning oligarchy; that of Shakespeare is not simply to be explained by the stage of incipient bourgeois capitalism to which he belonged. So Marx avoids saying that literature is only of interest to the age that produces it; society, he suggests, develops in a way that is analogous to the maturing of an individual human being, and we may take pleasure in, say, the Greeks' vivid rendering of the 'childhood' of civilisation, even though we recognise that it is irretrievably of the era that produced it. Implicit, however, in the whole of Marx's approach is the idea that recent and contemporary literature – being products of essentially the same socio-economic circumstances as the reader – is likely to be of most use and interest to a thinking man.

The impact of Marx's writings on world affairs has been so large that 'Marxist' thinking on literature goes far beyong what he himself wrote on the subject. We may identify two main fields of discussion provoked by Marxist theories:

1. If the most significant fact about literature is that it is a product of the society from which it emerged, are there any grounds for arguing that any one piece of literature is better (that is to say, more interesting, valuable, lasting or whatever) than another? Very crudely, can we say that *King Lear* is any more valuable than this morning's newspaper? What is the special role or value of the creative artist?

2. If literature inevitably reflects the social and economic development of society, is there a case for valuing authors of the past in terms of the ways they may be said to have encouraged or tried to retard that development? And should present-day writers be free to write as and what they please, given that social development has overwhelming political priority?

These questions have been posed most pointedly in some Marxist regimes, notably Stalinist Russia, where a literature of 'socialist realism' was deemed most appropriate to reflect the progress and achievements of the proletarian revolution; other types of literature – notably lyric poetry on themes of love and religion – were condemned as self-indulgent, bourgeois and reactionary. This regimentation of literature in terms of what is deemed to be useful to the state is no more in essence than what Plato advocated in his ideal Republic. Even in countries which are not politically committed to Marxism, this line of thinking has led to the widespread assumption that all art – whether explicitly political in theme or not – is a form of propaganda, and, whatever other qualities it may also have, may be judged as such. This assumption has led to long-running debates, for example, on the works of such authors as Yeats, Lawrence* and T. S. Eliot, which have been attacked for latent right-wing or fascist tendencies even though they are not overtly political in nature.

You do not have to be a committed Marxist to believe that Marxist thinking on literature has something useful to offer. One implicit danger in Romantic theories of literature was a tendency to exclusivism: the poet was a uniquely gifted individual, creating uniquely truthful art (for, as some were to develop the argument at the beginning of the twentieth century, an élite readership of specially qualified people). Marxism was surely useful in countering this tendency, and expanding the field of what might be considered significant literature – particularly in respect of the novel and certain kinds of drama (for example, that of Brecht†). A number of avowed Marxists have been first-rate critics, notably G. Lukacs‡ (*The Historical Novel; Studies in European Realism*) and Jean-Paul Sartre** (*What is Literature?*); even more fine critics have been inspired by Marxist theories without being committed to all their tenets – notably, in America, Edmund Wilson (1895–1972) (*Axel's Castle*, 1931; *To the Finland Station*, 1940) and Lionel Trilling (1905–75) (*The Liberal Imagination*, 1950); in Britain, George Orwell (1903–50) (*Collected Essays*, 1968) and Raymond Williams (*b.*1921) (*Culture and Society, 1780–1950*, 1958; *The Long Revolution*, 1961).

Sigmund Freud was interested in literature because he acknowledged the great authors of the past to be intuitive psychologists, offering

*William Butler Yeats (1865–1939), the Irish poet, dramatist and critic, was largely responsible for the Irish literary renaissance and was a founder of the Abbey Theatre. David Herbert Lawrence (1885–1930), the English novelist and poet, was the author of *Sons and Lovers* (1913), *The Rainbow* (1915) and *Women in Love* (1920).
†Berthold Brecht (1898–1956), the German poet and dramatist, was notable for his theories of stage presentation.
‡György Lukacs (1885–1971), the Hungarian Marxist philosopher and literary critic, whose works were first translated into English in 1962 and 1964.
**Jean Paul Sartre (1905–80), the French philosopher, novelist and critic; *What is Literature?* was translated into English in 1944.

occasional insights into the human mind, and particularly its unconscious dimension, which his own theory of psychoanalysis was to achieve on a more regular and scientific basis. Authors were among 'the few to whom it is vouchsafed . . . with hardly any effort to salvage from the whirlpool of their emotions the deepest truth to which we others have to force our way, ceaselessly groping among torturing uncertainties' (*Civilization and Its Discontents*, 1930). He suggested that this gift came to authors because literature, the creation of a fantasy life, offered an outlet to erotic impulses which would otherwise be thwarted or repressed; writing was thus a kind of therapy for those with neurotic tendencies. In it they revealed the desires of their unconscious minds, but usually distorted, fictionalised, distanced, in some way acceptable to the conscious mind, which always seeks – he maintained – to inhibit such self-revelation. Freud argued that the most powerful erotic drive in a man is to make love to his mother and kill the father who stands in his way – a pattern of behaviour most famously embodied in Sophocles's play, *Oedipus Tyrannus*, and so called by Freud the Oedipus complex. The fact that Sophocles's character acts in ignorance of the true facts of his parentage reflects, says Freud, the situation that the adult is not consciously aware of the oedipal drive, while the oracle's prediction of his actions suggests the inevitability of the whole process, given such deep-seated impulses.

Freud is almost exclusively concerned with the content of literature and has nothing to say about its style, genre or formal structure. Literature moves or attracts us, he maintains, because it deals symbolically with patterns of emotional experience which are common to all of us, or rather to all members of each sex, since the erotic drives of men differ from those of women; the Electra complex in women, for example, complements the Oedipus complex in men. Freud's theories do, however, lend extra currency to the important term, 'symbol', which was widely used by critics from Coleridge, through Yeats, to Eliot, and most particularly by the 'Symbolist' poets in France in the 1860s. The term was used in a variety of special senses, but the key suggestion was usually that language as used by the creative artist does not literally depict reality but somehow embodies key beliefs, ideas or concepts *about* reality in a particularly charged or effective way. The Freudian distinction between conscious and unconscious areas of the mind offers an explanation of how this might work: words which, on a conscious level, may simply seem to describe a character or scene or experience may trigger off echoes at an unconscious level, tapping or channeling some deep emotional impulse. Such a theory might encourage some writers to minimise the representational/mundane/literal elements in their work in order to concentrate on those parts of literature which may be deemed to speak as directly as possible to the unconscious mind.

Something of this is evident in the works of the Imagists and Modernists at the beginning of the twentieth century, though it is instructive to bear in mind that D. H. Lawrence, a writer who might seem to reflect many Freudian ideas, insisted that he had many reservations about Freud's theories as a whole.

Freud himself offers no explanation of why some works should be better or more moving than others, though he recognises that this is so; it is simply a mystery of the creative act. As he says of Dostoevsky,* a writer particularly close in spirit to his ideas, 'Before the problem of the creative artist, analysis must lay down its arms' ('Dostoevsky and Parricide'). His followers, however, quickly jumped to the conclusion that the most worthwhile literature is that which reflects the Oedipal or Electra complex most fully and faithfully. The most famous demonstration of this proposition is Ernest Jones's (1879–1958) *Hamlet and Oedipus* (1949), which draws many suggestive parallels between Shakespeare's play and *Oedipus Tyrannus*. There is a common misconception to the effect that Freudians such as Jones attempt to 'psychoanalyse' literary characters such as Hamlet as if they were real people. But this is not the case; inasmuch as a work of literature reflects a particular Oedipus complex, it is that of the author and not of his characters – Shakespeare not Hamlet, Sophocles not Oedipus.

As a literary critical tool, one weakness of the Freudian approach tends to be its capacity for ignoring many of the particular details and idiosyncracies of a text. Freudian critics tend to demonstrate the general adherence of the text to universal psychological truths rather than consider specific characteristics. This is also true of the literary criticism that derives from Freud's rivals and successors, notably the Austrian psychiatrist Alfred Adler (1870–1927) and the Swiss psychiatrist C. J. Jung (1875–1961). Adler rejected Freud's emphasis on sex, arguing that the struggle for power was the principal motivating force in man's make-up and introducing the superiority and inferiority complexes – which might be reflected in literature in just the same way as the Oedipus complex. Jung's idea of a racial 'collective unconscious', deriving from his study of myths and dreams, has been very influential in some literary circles; it has meshed with the work of many social anthropologists and helped to give some credence to the idea of the literary artist as a 'shaman' – a 'priest' or 'priest-doctor', invested with the special role of maintaining the spiritual health of the tribe or civilisation. (See, for example, Ted Hughes's *Gaudete*, 1977).

*Fyodor Dostoevsky (1821–81), the Russian novelist, author of *Crime and Punishment* (1866) and *The Brothers Karamazov* (1879–80).

Henry James	1843–1916

Despite the start made by Fielding, no serious theoretical criticism of the novel appeared in English until the end of the nineteenth century. Novels were reviewed, of course; Sir Walter Scott (1771–1832), the Scottish novelist, poet and historian who originated the historical novel, gave a generous reception to Jane Austen's *Emma* in the *Quarterly Review*, 1816, and George Eliot's* reviews are notable in their own right. But the major English novelists – Jane Austen, Scott, Dickens,† Thackeray‡ – did not have the same *theoretical* interest in the novel and its potential as their French counterparts (Balzac, Flaubert,** Zola). And major Romantic critics such as Coleridge and Arnold barely deigned to notice the novel as art; Arnold's late essay on Tolstoy has a good deal to say about the man and his thinking but nothing about the *art* of his novels ('the truth is that we are not to take Anna Karénine as a work of art; we are to take it as a piece of life').

Henry James's distinction as a critic lies in rescuing English fiction from this neglect, in insisting upon the novel as art rather than as a slice of life: 'only a short time ago it might have been supposed that the English novel was not what the French call *discutable*. It had no air of having a theory, a conviction, a consciousness of itself behind it – of being the expression of an artistic faith, the result of choice and comparison' ('The Art of Fiction', 1884). He insisted, in terms reminiscent of Coleridge, that the novel must be thought of as 'a living thing, all one and continuous, like any other organism, and in proportion as it lives will it be found, I think, that in each of the parts there is something of each of the other parts'. His chief method of demonstrating the art of writers' works is to outline their unique individuality of style, tone and vision, their artistic, but *not* biographical, personalities:

> Why is it that the life that overflows in Dickens seems to me always to go on in the morning, or in the very earliest hours of the afternoon at most, and in a vast apartment that appears to have windows, large, uncurtained, and rather unwashed windows, on all sides at once? Why is it that in George Eliot the sun sinks forever in the west, and the shadows are long, and the afternoon wanes, and the trees vaguely rustle, and the colour of the day is much inclined to yellow? Why is it

*The pen-name of Mary Anne Evans (1819–80); the great Victorian novelist, author of *The Mill on the Floss* (1860) and *Middlemarch* (1871–2).
†Charles Dickens (1812–70); see Part 3.
‡William Makepeace Thackeray (1811–63), the author of *Vanity Fair* (1847–8), *Pendennis* (1848), *Henry Esmond* (1852) and *The Newcomes* (1853–5).
**Gustave Flaubert (1821–81), the French novelist, author of *Madame Bovary* (1857).

that in Charlotte Brontë we move through an endless autumn? Why is it that in Jane Austen we sit quite resigned in an endless spring? ('The Lesson of Balzac', 1905).

In the prefaces to his own novels James has more to say about the techniques of fiction which create the 'personality' of the author here described so impressionistically; he addresses in particular the questions of perspective and of guiding the readers' attention through the story: 'The centre of interest throughout *Roderick [Hudson]* is in Rowland Mallet's consciousness, and the drama is the very drama of that consciousness – which I had to make sufficiently acute in order to enable it, like a set and lighted scene, to hold the play' (Preface to *Roderick Hudson*, 1875). The preface to *The Golden Bowl* (1904) outlines the theory of multiple perspectives in the novel. His ideal novel would use the 'discrimination and selection' of art to demonstrate what is significant in the 'inclusion and confusion' of life (Preface to *The Spoils of Poynton*, 1897). It is clear, though James is chary of spelling this out, that the art of the novel for him is not merely a matter of technique, of manipulating point of view; the principles of 'discrimination and selection' are ultimately based in morality – not a morality of specific codes and rules but one which insists that human life itself is valuable, and which finds the novel the most compatible of literary forms, being uniquely qualified in its scope and style to reflect and express that value. This dual stress on form and morality in the novel makes Henry James a key figure in the development of novel criticism, a precursor both of those critics such as the British critic Percy Lubbock (1879–1965) (*The Craft of Fiction*, 1921) and the American Wayne C. Booth (*b.*1921) (*The Rhetoric of Fiction*, 1961) who have concentrated on questions of narrative technique, and of those such as D. H. Lawrence ('Why the Novel Matters', 1936) and F. R. Leavis (*The Great Tradition*, 1948) who have primarily been interested in the novel as the genre in which the vitality of civilisation could best be discussed.

T. S. Eliot	1888–1965

It would be difficult to deny Eliot's place as the most influential critic of his generation. But it would be equally difficult to explain or justify it. In an age of mass popular culture, experiments in liberal democracy and widespread agnosticism, Eliot declared himself to be 'a classicist in literature, an Anglo-Catholic in religion, and a royalist in politics' (Preface to *For Lancelot Andrewes*, 1928). His essays disdain both the strain of academic argument and the detailed 'close reading' of so much twentieth-century criticism; they are fastidiously anti-Romantic in both style and content, often wickedly provocative – 'not that Montaigne had any philosophy whatsoever' is a famous throw-away parenthesis –

addressed primarily to a narrow audience of would-be fellow poets rather than the common reader, and occasionally just too cryptic for their own good.

Eliot's criticism parallels his own poetry in an oblique but revealing way. The early general essay, 'Tradition and the Individual Talent' (1919), sketches out many ideas which were to be developed later both in his poems and in more local pieces of criticism. He seeks to rebut the Romantic emphasis on the 'originality' and 'personality' of the poet as the most important feature of literature; the most vital features of poetry for him are those which contribute to the great tradition of European literature: 'not only the best, but the most individual parts of [a poet's] work may be those in which the dead poets, his ancestors, assert their immortality most vigorously.' This is not a plea for a slavish imitation of the past, but for a hard-won involvement in a real sense of history: 'Tradition . . . involves . . . the historical sense, which we may call nearly indispensable to anyone who would continue to be a poet beyond his twenty-fifth year; and the historical sense involves a perception, not only of the pastness of the past, but of its presence . . . .' Eliot looks for an almost mystical blending of the temporal and the timeless in the poet's perception, a sense that past and present confront each other endlessly; each new work adds to – and at the same time redefines – a tradition which is so much greater than the individuals who contribute to it. The art of the poet is thus not one of self-expression but one of self-denial: 'the progress of the artist is a continual self-sacrifice, a continual extinction of personality.' His private experiences and emotions may have nothing to do with his poetry at all, he argues, directly attacking Wordsworth's 'emotion recollected in tranquillity' formula: 'Poetry is not a turning loose of emotion but an escape from emotion; it is not expression of personality but an escape from personality. But, of course, only those who have personality and emotions know what it means to want to escape from these things.' This last sentence is a good example of what we may call Eliot's cryptic waspishness.

Paradoxically, this attack on the Romantic notion of the poet's special 'personality' leads not to the quasi-democracy of the neoclassical critics' view that anyone might be a poet if he follows Nature and the rules properly, but to an even more exclusive sense of the creative act taking place near-mystically on the borders of time and eternity, in the perfectly-tuned mind of a self-abnegating individual. There is an undeniable strain of contempt here, as often elsewhere in Eliot, for lesser mortals who cannot be expected to understand such things. It goes without saying that relatively few works of literature will be worthy of consideration in this view of what constitutes an artistic tradition – though one of them will surely be his own *The Waste Land* (1922), which reads as if written to justify 'Tradition and the Individual Talent'. When

Eliot's essays do consider specific authors and works it is almost always implicitly to assess their place in this special sense of the 'tradition', as potential models or *exempla* for the modern poet. The 'tradition' is self-consciously European and not just English (Dante, Pascal, Baudelaire*), but he writes most frequently about the English poets and dramatists of the sixteenth and seventeenth centuries – those who wrote before what, in 'The Metaphysical Poets' (1921), he calls 'a dissociation of sensibility' took place. (See below, pp. 91–2, on Donne's *Songs and Sonets.*) He wrote very little about the novel; this probably reflects his preference for the forms – poetry and drama – which had survived from classical times, and possibly also his distaste for 'popular culture'.

A number of Eliot's bewitching phrases, such as the 'objective correlative' which he concludes to be missing from *Hamlet* ('*Hamlet*', 1919), have passed into the general currency of criticism and Eliot remains the standard starting-point for most modern discussions of Elizabethan and Jacobean literature. But it is clearer now than perhaps it was thirty years ago that Eliot's criticism was as much a product of its time and place as any other; it was very much a part of the Modernist revolt against both the Romanticism and the liberal historical criticism of the nineteenth century, its conservatism sharpened by a widespread feeling that the First World War had marked a crucial phase in the decline of European culture. It has been common to think of Eliot as the father-figure of modern literary criticism, but it may be more accurate to think of him as the last major figure in the line of poet-critics (Jonson, Dryden, Johnson, Coleridge, Arnold) for whom poetry and criticism have been complementary routes to a definition of what matters in our culture.

New Criticism

Criticism in the twentieth century has differed from all that went before for the simple reason that it has become a university (and latterly school) subject. The enormous growth in the practice of criticism in the period can be attributed to this fact, as can the appearance of innumerable periodical journals solely or largely devoted to literary criticism in all its various modes and emphases. Many established branches of criticism – historical, biographical, Marxist, generic, for example – have continued to flourish in this new climate, though all have been obliged to re-scrutinise their credentials. But in the period from, approximately, 1925 to 1960 various new approaches emerged, in direct response to the demands of teaching criticism, which it may be useful to consider together under the heading of 'New Criticism'. This label was actually

---

*Blaise Pascal (1623–62), the French scientist and religious philosopher, author of *Pensées* (1669); Charles Baudelaire (1821–67), the French poet, author of *Les Fleurs du Mal* (1857).

adopted as a polemical banner by a number of American critics in the late 1930s and 1940s, one of whom, John Crowe Ransom (1888–1974), used it for the title of a book – *The New Criticism* – in 1941; they founded what amounted to a 'school' of criticism, with a set of principles that became more fixed and definite as its members became more established in the academic world. But New Criticism may be said to have had its roots earlier than this in England, and more specifically in Cambridge, although, rather typically, there it never settled into a definite 'school' with a fixed theoretical programme.

Many New Critics, on both sides of the Atlantic, looked to Eliot as a guiding spirit, but less as an example of how to write criticism than as a demonstration that the study of literature – past and present – could still be significant even when divorced from the Romantic emphasis on the 'poetic personality' and the Victorian obsession with history. If Eliot was the guiding spirit, the trail-blazer of the new critical theories was I. A. Richards, whose books, *The Principles of Literary Criticism* (1924) and *Practical Criticism* (1929) have had a profound effect on the teaching of literature. Richards's original interests were in aesthetics and psychology, and his most influential contributions to criticism have been attempts to define the validity of literary value-judgements and to assess the reading process itself in the quasi-scientific terms of communications theory. For the latter he conducted 'laboratory' experiments on his students at Cambridge, giving them copies of unfamiliar poems on which he asked them to comment freely; his analysis of their responses, in *Practical Criticism*, revealed wholesale inadequacies, which he listed under ten heads, ranging from simple incomprehension to inhibition and sentimentality. He concluded that the state of literacy was outrageously low in England – he was assuming, of course, that his Cambridge students ought to be among the best readers – and that the teaching of literature needed to be reformed to encourage much more accurate responses to texts. It is questionable whether such a 'laboratory' experiment would really test the *normal* reading process at all – we do not normally approach texts in a clinical vacuum. It is, moreover, open to doubt whether the inadequacies described reflected *reading* difficulties on the part of the students, or their inability to *express* what they had made of the texts. Nevertheless, this set the norm for later New Critical thinking: the text in isolation was all that mattered, and the role of the critic was detailed exegesis of the words on the printed page.

Richards's choice of poems for his experiment, and relatively brief ones at that, also foreshadowed another feature of what was to come. Such close scrutiny, as it were in a vacuum, put a premium on literature with certain qualities, many of which were spelled out by the English critic and poet William Empson (*b*.1906), a pupil of Richards, in *Seven*

Types of Ambiguity (1930). Empson attempts to define the 'difficulty' or flexible meaning of poetry in terms of its 'ambiguity' ('any verbal nuance, however slight, which gives room for alternative reactions') which he distinguished in seven types, representing 'stages of advancing logical disorder'. This helped to give currency to many of the stock terms of New Criticism – 'ambiguity' itself, 'irony', and 'tension', that is, the tension between words in the generation of meaning. It was recognised immediately that the kinds of texts which most readily repaid the search for such qualities were generally those which Eliot had praised on rather different grounds – for example, Shakespeare's sonnets and the lyrics of the Metaphysical poets – though Eliot himself was sceptical of what he called 'the lemon-squeezer school of criticism'. Many larger works seemed deficient when measured by these standards, particularly long narrative poems such as those of Spenser and Milton; so too did much of the reflective poetry of the nineteenth century. But it was found that the plays of Shakespeare and some other Elizabethans could be treated as 'dramatic poems', essentially by ignoring their status as performance-texts, and this helped to preserve their status for New Criticism; interest focused on the way that they were bound together on a verbal level by recurrent threads of imagery, which helped to identify them as organically perfect artefacts (see, for example, Derek Traversi, *An Approach to Shakespeare*, 1938). Not all critics, however, who were interested in Shakespearean imagery-analysis subscribed wholeheartedly to New Critical premises – it was a tool which could be put to a variety of uses. (See the comments below on Caroline Spurgeon and G. Wilson Knight in the section on *Macbeth*, pp. 84–5.)

The difficulty of confining New Criticism to a 'school', particularly in England, is demonstrated by the fact that Empson, in his next book, *Some Versions of Pastoral* (1935) develops the concept of 'ambiguity' in relation to much more substantial texts and in so doing ventures into Marxist and Freudian modes of criticism which are anathema to the strict New Critic. Similarly, the most influential of all English critics who were associated with the early Eliot, Richards and Empson – F. R. Leavis – was at best only tangentially a New Critic. In *Revaluation* (1936), Leavis argued that 'the rule of the critics is, or should (I think) be, to work as much as possible in terms of particular analysis – analysis of poems or passages – and to say nothing that cannot be related immediately to judgements about producible texts'. And this was the 'rule' that was followed in *Scrutiny*, the highly influential periodical he ran from 1932 to 1953. But exegesis was never, for Leavis, merely an end in itself, as it sometimes seemed to be for American New Critics; it was a way of looking for certain qualities in literature which he considered most significant. In the first instance it was those qualities in poetry which Eliot had most approved of – a fusion of passion and intelligence, sensuous particularity in the use of language, a sense of tradition. *New Bearings in English Poetry* (1932) traced such qualities in Eliot's own poetry, and in that of the American poet Ezra Pound (1885–1972) and Gerard Manley Hopkins (1884–99), the English Jesuit and poet, but failed to find them – and denounced their absence – in the works of other late Victorians, Yeats and the 'Georgian' poets. *Revaluation* looked back into history for the same qualities and found them mainly in Donne and the Metaphysicals, also in Pope, but only intermittently in the Romantics. Later, Leavis developed an Arnold-style concern for the state of English culture as a whole – the study of literature virtually replacing the study of theology as the highest critical endeavour of civilisation. His attention switched, in *The Great Tradition* (1948), to the great tradition of the novel – for him, Jane Austen, George Eliot, Henry James, Joseph Conrad (1857–1924), the Polish-born English novelist, and D. H. Lawrence, (who was dealt with separately in *D. H. Lawrence: Novelist* (1955) – all writers whose works were distinguished, he insisted, by a vital morality in their view of life.

It was left to the Americans to expound New Criticism as a fully-fledged theoretical system. In the United States Cleanth Brooks (*b*.1906) and Robert Penn Warren (*b*.1905) edited a much-used college anthology, *Understanding Poetry* (1938) which they declared in the preface to be 'conceived on the assumption that if poetry is worth teaching at all, it is worth teaching as poetry' – not as evidence of some historical, biographical or moral truth. Similarly Brooks's collection of essays, *The Well-Wrought Urn* (1947) – the title is a revealing allusion to Donne's poem, 'The Canonization' – scrupulously avoids historical perspectives in its insistence on the text-as-text. Many of the basic assumptions of New Criticism are synthesised in René Wellek (*b*.1903, in Austria) and Austen Warren's (*b*.1899, in the U.S.) *Theory of Literature* (1949), while its fullest theoretical defence is made in two articles by the American critics W. K. Wimsatt Jr (*b*.1907) and Monroe C. Beardsley (*b*.1915), 'The Intentional Fallacy' and 'The Affective Fallacy', both collected in Wimsatt's *The Verbal Icon* (1954). The former article argues that 'the design or intention of the author is neither available not desirable as a standard for judging the success of a work of literary art' while the latter exposes the 'fallacy' of 'trying to derive the standard of criticism from the psychological effect of the poem' since this must end 'in impressionism and relativism'. The text, and nothing but the text, is all.

The New Criticism obviously had many attractions in the schoolroom; there was no mass of extrinsic material to be learned about authors, influences, historical movements or genres before getting down to business; the text was open to all and every critic had equal access – the only key he might need or be allowed being a substantial

dictionary; it was relatively easy to compare one critical performance
with another – the most 'complex' or 'difficult' reading of any text being
implicitly the most impressive. There is no doubt that it raised the
standard of literacy as Richards defined it in *Practical Criticism* and
enormously sharpened responses to one of our general questions: 'How
does a piece of literature work?' But it had no explicit answer to the other
question: 'What is the value of literature?' It assumed implicitly that
whatever succumbed most readily to its own methodology must be best,
unless, as with Leavis, a set of moral imperatives was silently adduced to
supplement the apparently objective 'common pursuit of true
judgement' – Eliot's phrase, borrowed for the title of a book. New
Criticism could be silly, like any critical theory carried to extremes, as,
for example, when its most extreme adherents refused to admit that a
word's changing sense down the ages should be taken into account when
reading a text, arguing that what it means *now* is all that matters. This
would, for instance, eliminate half the sexual innuendo in Shakespeare
and Donne. More generally, it has been objected that the kinds of irony,
ambiguity and nuance which the New Critics admired in literature are
qualities most likely to appeal to people of a certain type of
background – sophisticated, well-read, articulate. On the other hand,
New Criticism was surely not wrong in insisting that the reader's
attention should *primarily* be on the text: we can only begin to ask the
broader questions about the value of a text – how it relates, say, to its
author, age or genre – when we have examined in detail what it actually
says and how it says it.

Newer than New: stylistics and structuralism

New Criticism was always an unfortunate label, like that of the
Modernism from which, in some respects, it grew: there would soon be a
time when it was no longer new or modern. In the past thirty years there
have been any number of attempts to break out of the apparent *impasse*
of the New Critical fixation with the text. One example, which has no
general label but is easily identifiable in the development of university
departments of Theatre Arts and Theatre Studies, is the insistence that
plays are not 'dramatic poems' but can best be understood (some would
say 'only be understood') as texts for performance – in the context of the
history and theory of the theatre. This has not only enriched our
understanding of the classical canon of drama (see, for example, the
American critic Marvin Rosenberg's (*b*.1912) studies of the major
Shakespearean tragedies, mentioned below in the section on *Macbeth*,
p. 86), but has greatly expanded concepts of what constitutes legitimate drama – finding value, for instance, in street, fringe, tribal
and folk theatre, mime and the musical, all of them significant in their

own right, but also helping to illuminate the great stage classics. The best-known figure in this general movement is the British theatre director, Peter Brook (*b*.1925); see his *The Empty Space*, 1968. The current unresolved question is whether the development of 'theatre studies' takes the study of drama out of literary criticism, where it has been since Aristotle, altogether, to form a separate discipline, or whether literary criticism can respond to the challenge by absorbing something from the new approach or asserting equally valid approaches of its own.

These developments in respect of drama are symptomatic of other advances in critical theory, many of which are associated with what we may broadly call communications theory, an amalgam of insights from linguistics, sociology and psychology. We can identify in *stylistics* and *structuralism* two approaches that have proved fruitful, though it is not always easy to say where one ends and the other begins.

'Style' has been widely used as a term in criticism for centuries, often in a rather impressionistic way, in attempts to draw attention to the characteristic or peculiar use of language in a particular text, author or period. Modern 'stylistics' is an attempt to approach the question of style on stricter, more methodical lines; it is not so much a discipline in itself as a cross-over point between linguistics, for which literary texts are only one item of interest in the broad study of language, and literary criticism. It starts from the proposition that any idea or concept may be expressed in one of a number of different ways, and that an author exercises a choice (conscious or unconscious; dictated by personal taste or the demands of the reader, genre or whatever) in determining the precise form of words to be used. Such a proposition is, incidentally, anathema to New Criticism, which refuses to distinguish between the form and content of literature: what is written is written.

Literary stylistics poses for itself the task of assessing and classifying the range of linguistic choice available to authors, identifying the ways in which features of the linguistic 'surface' of a text may call attention to themselves: they may, for example, deviate from some accepted norm in their manner of expression, or in other ways be 'foregrounded' (a key term in literary stylistics). These classifications may then be applied to a particular text, or number of texts, in such a way as to highlight their peculiar verbal characteristics. Such a procedure may be put to a variety of uses: for example, building up evidence to confirm or deny our impressionistic sense that certain features of style are characteristic of certain forms or periods in literature (see, for example, the American philologist and critic Josephine Miles (*b*.1911), *Eras and Modes in English Poetry*, 1957, 1964). More controversially, it may even be used in an attempt to isolate a particular author's 'literary fingerprints', perhaps with a view to determining the authorship of anonymous or disputed texts. But this procedure is most directly useful to literary criticism when it is applied to texts in such a way as to demonstrate that they are not merely verbal constructions, as New Criticism often implies, nor are they pure sets of messages, that is, pure semantic information,* but something uniquely in between – examples of what stylistics calls 'discourse'. The mode of discourse adopted by the author for his text will largely determine the way in which it is apprehended by a reader; and so the more closely we can explain and quantify that mode the closer we are to explaining, or demonstrating, how that text 'works'.

Stylistics does not offer to replace literary criticism as it has been known in the past, but it does offer some refinements to it. Most exponents of literary stylistics are prepared to acknowledge that the texts which they choose to submit to their characteristic method of analysis are interesting or valuable *firstly* for any number of reasons that may barely be touched upon by that analysis; stylistics helps merely to describe the distinctively linguistic dimension of that interest or value. A New Critic who, shall we say, offered a cogent reading of some long-neglected poem might hope thereby to make his readers re-evaluate it; a critic employing stylistic methodology could only really hope to make them see it afresh by getting them to focus on its constituent linguistic features. The final business of appreciating literature remains when stylistics has had its say.

So stylistics may be of most use to the critic in offering him a vocabulary to describe precisely details of verbal nuance and presentation – without submitting to the artificial constraints of New Criticism (far from putting the text in a vacuum, stylistics compares it with as many other uses of language as possible) and without favouring certain kinds of verbal richness – such as ambiguity, irony, paradox and so on – over others. Stylistics does, however, have one drawback in common with New Criticism: 'linguistic techniques are more readily adapted to the miniature exegesis of a lyric poem, than the examination of a full-scale novel. In prose, the problem of how to select – what sample passages, what features to study – is more acute, and the incompleteness of even the most detailed analysis more apparent'†. One other feature of stylistics regretted by more traditional critics is its recourse to a special vocabulary, most of it imported from linguistics; it has been likened to the vocabulary of the old classical rhetoric, with which stylistics has much in common. It is regrettable because it tends to form a barrier between critics who choose to use this special terminology

*Semantics is the general term applied to the study of meaning; 'semantic information' means the ideas and the significance of a communication divorced from the forms (the words, pictures, and so on) in which it was delivered.
†G. N. Leech and M. H. Short, *Style in Fiction: a Linguistic Introduction to English Fictional Prose*, 1981, p. 3.

and those who do not; in a wider context, it definitely creates a barrier between criticism and the general reading public. The private language of stylistics announces it to be a quasi-science, distinctively a university discipline, and scarcely the concern of the general reader, much less the average writer; to many people this seems an unfortunate price to have to pay for the real benefits that stylistics can offer criticism.

If stylistics has, for these reasons, been greeted with some circumspection, particularly in England, how much more is this true of *structuralism*. This is a phenomenon which it is difficult to divorce, in its application to literary criticism, from *semiotics* or *semiology*, which is the science of signs. The former term is generally preferred in the United States, in deference to its originator, the American physicist and logician C. S. Pierce (1839–1941); the latter in Europe, following the Swiss linguist Ferdinand de Saussure (1857–1913). Structuralism is the name given to a twentieth-century body of thinking which fundamentally challenges everyday Western European concepts of 'reality'; it starts from the proposition (intelligible enough in the wake of the fundamental assaults on our understanding of man, society and the universe made by Darwin, Marx, Freud and Einstein) that the world is not made up of independent objects that are knowable and classifiable in absolute terms. Things only really exist inasmuch as we perceive them, and the act of perception is governed by innumerable factors which make objectivity impossible: so, to some significant extent, we create what we perceive. It follows that all we can really know is the *relationship* between the observer and the thing observed; this is the stuff of 'reality'. It further follows that no thing or experience is inherently significant, but only so when it is comprehended in the set of relationships, the structure, of which it forms a part.

In this view of things, the process of signification, that is, making signs which imply meaning, is much more widespread than is commonly supposed; all human social behaviour – eating, sport, wearing clothes or perfume, politics, telling stories, whatever – is a process of making signs about our relationship with the world. Much 'structuralist' thinking, such as that of the anthropologist Claude Lévi-Strauss, is devoted to uncovering the underlying 'rules' by which this process of sign-making in society is able to operate. Oral and written languages are only particular ways in which such signs are made; and literature is only one way of using languages.

The signs we make, including literature, are thus not intelligible because they refer to some objective reality, which is non-existent or at least non-discernible, but because they correspond to the process of discerning relationships ('structuring') by which we, as it were, create the reality we inhabit. This process presumably derives from the operation of the brain itself, about which little is known for certain. The key assumption is that we build up our sense of structures from an observation of binary oppositions, that is, very basic contrasting relationships, between things – red and green, for example, or circles and squares. These mean nothing in themselves, but they can acquire significance or meaning within a total structure (for instance, red means 'stop' and green means 'go'). This meaning will only be intelligible to the culture or society which has assented to that particular structure. We can observe this in the operation of language itself; words, at least in Western European languages, do not normally *represent* the phenomena they discuss. There is nothing either in the sounds or the shape of the word 'house' in English (or *maison* in French, or *domus* in Latin) which *means* a building of bricks, stone or timber for living in; the words only acquire that meaning when employed within the intelligible structures, the languages, of which they form a part.

Saussure tried to explain how this operates in practice by distinguishing between *langue* and *parole*. The former, in English, means approximately 'language', as we might use it in the phrase, 'the English language'; it is an abstract set of rules or conventions about the way we communicate within our society. *Parole* means 'speech', everyday examples of the use of words. Looked at in isolation, individual examples of *parole* seem chaotic or formless; they only take on meaning, and so communicate, because they subscribe to the rules of the *langue* of the particular community or society. Saussure cites the analogy of a game of chess; any particular game only makes sense in relation to the mutually accepted rules and conventions, in effect the structure, governing all such games; the analogy would hold true for any recognised sport. A major preoccupation of linguistics in this century has been an attempt to work through *parole* to a definition of the universal terms of *langue*.

In respect of literature, it may loosely be said that the central activity of structuralist critics has been to discern a *langue* of literature, to which individual texts stand as examples of *parole*. This is sometimes described as a search for a 'poetics' of literature. This goes back to Aristotle's term; it is not confined, of course, to literature in verse. To this extent, structuralist criticism may be seen as an extension of the approach to literature via genre, an attempt to come to terms with the way in which it communicates through its sheer 'literariness'. Northrop Frye's *Anatomy of Criticism* (1957) is a key work in this context. But a central tenet of many of those searching for a 'poetics' of literature, particularly of those writing in French, is that no text, no instance of literary *parole*, can be 'pure' or 'innocent' in its relation to the 'poetics' or literary *langue* by which it acquires meaning. Literature, like any other sign-system, is a way of registering perceptual relationships (and not, in any simplistic sense, 'reality'); but it is one that aims at understanding, and so controlling, the version of truth revealed in that process of registration. In so doing, it necessarily reveals its own capacity for *changing* the truth or reality it registers. For many structuralists, this is the most important feature of art, and of literature in particular; every choice of words, every choice of forms, implies the possibility of alternative choices of words and forms which would have 'created' alternative realities. (It should be apparent that the characteristic mode of structuralist analyses of texts can be very similar to that employed in stylistics – the detailed exegesis of linguistic features of the text in relation to other possible formulations; but the rationale behind it is implicitly very different.) In this capacity to imply alternative realities, all literature may be said to be revolutionary in its impact, however conservative its 'content' may appear to be; in the process of understanding its 'signs', the reader is made increasingly aware of the arbitrary way in which they operate, of the fact that they have no fixed connotation but may take on successive, theoretically infinite meanings, depending on our appreciation of the total structure. Thus they challenge us to construct our own new 'reality'. This helps to explain a general preference apparent in much structuralist criticism for the sort of writing – such as Sterne's *Tristram Shandy* and the works of the Irish authors James Joyce (1882–1941) and Samuel Beckett (*b*.1906) – which draws attention to the sheer arbitrariness of its own sign-system; such writing is implicitly more 'honest' than quasi-realistic literature. It also explains, however, why one of the major works of structuralist criticism so far – *S/Z*, by the French critic, Roland Barthes (Paris, 1970; English translation, 1974) – is single-mindedly dedicated to exposing what it sees as the imposture of 'realistic' novels, which it attempts in an exhaustive analysis of one short story, 'Sarrasine', by the notoriously 'realist' author, Balzac.

The implications of structuralism are far-reaching in many fields – not only linguistics and literature, but anthropology, sociology, psychology, economics, even physics. There can be little doubt that the sheer extent of its claims (a key to all connections?) has been one factor in making many English and American critics sceptical about it; like Marxism, it seductively pretends to have answers to all questions, but it is difficult to accept some of these answers without accepting them all. This is tied up with the fact that the difficult concepts with which structuralism attempts to deal have led to the adoption of extremely specialist jargon, some, but not all of it, overlapping with that employed in stylistics, often redefined by successive theorists to suit particular purposes. The suspicion is abroad that too much of structuralism is concerned with theoretical attempts to explain and define itself, at the expense of such items as the literary texts it offers to explicate. This suspicion is only reinforced by the existence of a variety of critical approaches such as formalism, phenomenology and deconstructionism which are clearly related to mainstream structuralism – if there is such a thing – but which lay claim to particular refinements and advantages.

A further problem has certainly been that, while in general terms structuralism seems to offer ways of examining literature dispassionately in the broadest context of culture and communication, so much actual structuralist criticism has had a radical, not to say revolutionary, bias, evaluating texts in terms of the ways in which they apparently defend or subvert the supposedly corrupt society which produced them. Where this political dimension has not been evident, a further implication has arisen, equally intimidating to some people, which is that literature is not *about* anything at all, except itself: that what matters about a text is the way its form and style come together to register a type of communication; that the author and his chosen subject-matter are only incidentals in an impersonal world where everything man-made may be said to communicate *something*. This may be a logically defensible argument, but common sense suggests that it is a long way removed from the reasons why most people bother to write or read literature. Most Anglo-Saxon critics have so far proved too empiricist in outlook to swallow the argument whole.

For all that, structuralism can clearly be useful in underlining the fact that literature is only one means of communication among many and in making us self-conscious about literature as a medium. In terms of the status they have been given in schools and in society as a whole, printed books have been the most influential means of communication and the most privileged medium in the Western world since the Renaissance: to what extent has this shaped our thinking about the world, indeed created our whole concept of 'reality'? We may remember that our history of literary criticism began with Plato, one of whose objections to books and the written word was that they were inherently less truthful than the forms of open-ended dialogue and debate which he had learned from his teacher, Socrates. Structuralism may yet offer us the best perspective for observing the struggle as film and television increasingly challenge the primacy of the written word and the printed page.*

This selective history has been written to demonstrate that there is no such thing as definitive literary criticism. Any approach can only ask a limited number of questions we may legitimately pose in our efforts to understand and appreciate literature. It is always a useful and instructive exercise to weigh up the relative strengths and weaknesses of the various approaches: which work better with certain kinds of texts than others, and why? Which seem more anxious to prove a general

---

*See Marshall McLuhan, *The Gutenberg Galaxy*, 1962; Terence Hawkes, *Structuralism and Semiotics*, 1977; R. Scholes, *Structuralism in Literature*, 1974; J. Culler, *Structuralist Poetics*, 1975).

proposition than to come to terms with particular texts? Which seek to tell you more about the author who wrote a text, or the age that produced it, or the genre to which it belongs, than they do about the text itself? And why? – what secret proposition are they trying to sell about the nature of literature? What is the small print in the contract they are trying to foist off on you?

A history of criticism can be an intimidating thing, bringing home to a reader just how much has been written and thought on the subject, apparently suggesting that there is nothing new left to be said. The history of criticism, however, demonstrates that the exact opposite is true: there is always something new to be said. The more literature is written, the more we change our perception of man, society and the nature of communication, the more scope there will be for new critical approaches – none of which will ever supplant those which have gone before but some of which may prove useful enough to supplement them.

An aspiring critic, therefore, should consider his options carefully and not commit himself too readily to any single approach. However attractive superficially, any approach can be reduced to silliness if applied with blind faith and without circumspection. For some indication of the potential pitfalls, see Frederick C. Crews's delightful *The Pooh Perplex* (1963), in which various critical approaches are applied (tongue-in-cheek) to A. A. Milne's (1882–1956) popular Pooh books for children; it would be a useful exercise to consider supplying your own chapters on some of the more recent 'schools' of criticism. There are no short-cuts to comprehending literature; there is no substitute for reading and re-reading a text, for thinking about it from as many perspectives as possible. But reading and thinking will be that much sharper and constructive if you are conscious of the ways that other critics have thought and read: that is the real justification for studying literary criticism.

Part 3

The critical fortunes of three major texts

THIS PART AIMS to complement Part 2 by giving some indication of how changing critical fashions have treated three specific texts – one from each of the major genres (drama, poetry and prose fiction): Shakespeare's *Macbeth*, Donne's *Songs and Sonets* and Dickens's *Great Expectations*. In the space available it has not been possible to give more than brief outlines of some lengthy and sophisticated arguments, and many significant points of view have had to be overlooked altogether. The intention is to give a general indication of the sheer range of critical approaches which have been deemed valid and useful in respect of each work, and of the scope for disagreement about each of them.

There are now collections of critical essays, bringing together a diversity of critical opinions, on most major authors and texts in English literature; see, for example, the 'Casebook' series published by Macmillan (London) and the 'Twentieth Century Views' series published by Prentice-Hall (Englewood Cliffs, New Jersey). It is an instructive exercise to read any one of these from cover to cover.

Macbeth by William Shakespeare

We know little about the contemporary reception of *Macbeth* (*c*.1606). It is generally supposed that its subject-matter of Scottish history and witchcraft would have appealed to King James I, who had a deep interest in witchcraft and was a Scot by birth; and the banquet scene in which Banquo's ghost appears seems to have made sufficient impact to be worth alluding to in two plays performed shortly after *Macbeth* (*The Puritaine* and *The Knight of the Burning Pestle*, both *c*.1607). Dr Simon Forman gives a detailed description of a performance of the play at the Globe Theatre in 1611, which suggests, at least, that the play was popular enough to be revived, but offers no criticism of it.* Implicit criticism came in 1674 when the dramatist Sir William D'Avenant (1606–68) – Shakespeare's supposed godson – 'adapted' Shakespeare's text in a version that held the stage until the notable actor David Garrick (1717–79) went back, more or less, to the original in 1744. This fate

---

*Simon Forman (1552–1611) was a physician and astrologer. His manuscript *Book of Plays* contains a number of eye-witness accounts of Shakespeare's plays. It is printed in E. K. Chambers, *William Shakespeare: a Study of Facts and Problems*, 2 vols., 1930.

commonly befell Shakespeare's plays in the Restoration, most famously in the Irish dramatist and poet laureate Nahum Tate's (1652–1717) adaptation of *King Lear*; the idea was to 'regularise' Shakespeare according to standards dictated by the supposed 'civility' of the age (see the section above on Dryden, pp. 36–7), and also to offer more scope for the actresses then allowed to perform on the stage for the first time. So, for example, D'Avenant inserted a dialogue between Lady Macbeth and Lady Macduff (I.v.) and a scene in which Lady Macbeth expresses her remorse (IV), making the moral point of the play more obvious; he also generally ironed out the 'irregularities' of Shakespeare's verse.

The first major criticism of *Macbeth* comes from Dr Johnson; his comments on its language, in *The Rambler* (1751), the periodical he edited from 1750 to 1752, are typical of Augustan taste:

When Macbeth is confirming himself in the horrid purpose of stabbing his king, he breaks out amidst his emotions into a wish natural to a murderer.

Come, thick night,

And pall thee in the dunnest smoke of hell,
That my keen knife see not the wound it makes,
Nor heaven peep through the blanket of the dark,
To cry, 'Hold, hold!'

In this passage is exerted all the force of poetry, that force which calls new powers into being, which embodies sentiment and animates matter; yet perhaps scarce any man now peruses it without some disturbance of his attention from the counteraction of the words to the ideas. What can be more dreadful than to implore the presence of the night, invested not in common obscurity, but in the smoke of hell? Yet the efficacy of this invocation is destroyed by the insertion of an epithet now seldom heard but in the stable, and *dun* night may come or go without any other notice than contempt ... we do not immediately conceive that any crime of importance is to be committed with a *knife* [described by Johnson as 'an instrument used by butchers and cooks in the meanest employments'] ... who, without some relaxation of his gravity, can hear of the avengers of guilt *peeping through a blanket*?

It is altogether typical of Johnson, who was given to quoting from memory, that he should have made the elementary blunder of ascribing this passage to Macbeth when it is actually spoken by Lady Macbeth; but this need not invalidate the general point that he is trying to make about what he sees as 'the counteraction of the words to the ideas'. The General Observation on *Macbeth* in his edition of Shakespeare does its best to assert the orthodox morality of the play, but can only be described as lacklustre in its other praises; it seems likely that the supernatural elements (the witches, ghost and so on) offended Johnson's Augustan common sense:

> This play is deservedly celebrated for the propriety of its fictions, and solemnity, grandeur, and variety of its actions; but it has no nice discriminations of character, the events are too great to admit the influence of particular dispositions, and the course of the action necessarily determines the conduct of the agents.
>
> The danger of ambition is well described; and I know not whether it may not be said in defense of some parts which now seem improbable, that, in Shakespeare's time, it was necessary to warn credulity against vain and illusive predictions.
>
> The passions are directed to their true end. Lady Macbeth is merely detested; and though the courage of Macbeth preserves some esteem, yet every reader rejoices at his fall.

Coming so shortly after Johnson's predictably neoclassical concern for the play's depiction of general and moral truths, the *Specimen of a Commentary on Shakespeare* (1794) by Walter Whiter (1758–1832), the English philologist and critic, was a remarkable pre-Romantic attempt to get inside the dramatist's mind by analysing his imagery according to the principles of John Locke's* 'association of ideas' theory; it offers an interesting refutation of Johnson's objections to 'Come, thick night' by showing the association of 'knife' and 'blanket' with the Elizabethan theatre. The whole work is much more sympathetic than earlier criticism had been to Shakespeare's playing with words and drawing on images from a wide range of experience. But the book went unnoticed and the idea of image-analysis it had pioneered lay dormant until the 1930s.

Coleridge's main comments on *Macbeth* occur in the notes he made in his copy of Shakespeare, for use in his lectures; they are patchy but offer interesting contrasts with Johnson. He finds Lady Macbeth, at least, firmly characterised:

> Lady Macbeth, like all in Shakespeare, is a class individualized: – of high rank, left much alone, and feeding herself with day-dreams of ambition, she mistakes the courage of fantasy for the power of bearing the consequences of the realities of guilt. Hers is the mock fortitude of a mind deluded by ambition; she shames her husband with a superhuman audacity of fancy which she cannot support, but sinks in the season of remorse, and dies in suicidal agony.

Such comments, bordering on speculation beyond the information actually supplied by the text, make Coleridge a key figure in the

*John Locke (1632–1704), the English philosopher, author of *Essay Concerning Human Understanding* (1690) and *Two Treatises of Civil Government* (1690).

character-analysis school of criticism. But even more influential were such comments as those he made about what he saw as the play's remarkably unified style (with one significant exception):

> Excepting the disgusting passage of the Porter, which I dare pledge myself to demonstrate an interpolation of the actors, I do not remember in *Macbeth* a single pun or play on words... Entire absence of comedy, nay, even of irony and philosophic contemplation in *Macbeth* – because wholly tragic.

The 'low porter soliloquy' clearly goes against Coleridge's view of what the true poetic Imagination (such as Shakespeare surely possessed) would produce in this play, though he detects the true Shakespearean touch in the 'primrose way' passage; he is neither the first nor the last critic to decide arbitrarily what he will accept as 'genuine' Shakespeare, but he is one of the most blatant:

> I believe [it] written for the mob by some other hand, perhaps with Shakespeare's consent – and that finding it take, he with the remaining ink of a pen otherwise employed just interpolated it with the sentence, 'I'll devil-porter it no further' and what follows to 'bonfire'. Of the rest not one syllable has the ever-present being of Shakespeare.

Later critics would disagree with Coleridge's judgement about this particular scene, but the fundamental concept that lies behind the judgement – the idea of the organic unity imposed on a work of art by the Imagination – remains a potent one to this day, not least in relation to Shakespeare.

Thomas De Quincey's (1785–1859) essay, 'On the Knocking on the Gate in *Macbeth*' (1823), pays similar Romantic homage to Shakespeare's seemingly casual but deeply informed artistry; he tries to explain why 'the knocking at the gate, which succeeds to the murder of Duncan, produced to my feelings an effect for which I could never account', goes on to argue that 'the re-establishment of the goings-on of the world in which we live, first makes us profoundly sensible of the awful parenthesis that had suspended them' and concludes 'O mighty poet ... the further we press in our discoveries, the more we shall see proofs of design and self-supporting arrangement where the careless eye had seen nothing but accident!' Had he known about it, De Quincey might have answered Coleridge's objection to the Porter scene as a whole with this argument, but in fact he did not.

Much nineteenth-century criticism of *Macbeth* followed the lead of the English essayist and critic William Hazlitt (1778–1830) in his *Characters of Shakespeare's Plays* (1817–18), in its concentration on the characters as the chief focus of interest. This culminated in A. C.

Bradley's (1851–1935) essay on the play in his enormously influential *Shakespearean Tragedy* (1904). After some comments on the play's 'special tone or atmosphere', Bradley devotes most of the essay to describing in detail 'the two great terrible figures who dwarf all the remaining characters of the drama. Both are sublime, and both inspire, far more than the other tragic heroes, the feeling of awe.' He writes consistently as if Shakespeare had managed total and exhaustive portraits of Macbeth and Lady Macbeth – or, if not total, sufficiently so that we may surmise the pieces he left out:

> The phrase . . . 'too full of the milk of human kindness', is applied to him in impatience by his wife, who did not fully understand him; but certainly he was far from devoid of humanity and pity . . . . At the same time he was exceedingly ambitious. He must have been so by temper. The tendency must have been greatly strengthened by his marriage.

It is as if Bradley was writing about real human beings rather than the characters defined within the play.

The classic reply to Bradley and the whole character-analysis approach to drama is L. C. Knights's (*b.*1906) essay, 'How Many Children Had Lady Macbeth?' (printed in his collection of essays, *Explorations*, 1933). This is less an analysis of *Macbeth* itself than a demonstration of the limitations and incongruities of taking dramatic characters as if they were real people, or even drawn from novels; the title derives mischievously from Lady Macbeth's admission (I.vii) that she has 'given suck' – a fact adduced by Shakespeare only so that she may express her current unwomanly feelings as strongly as possible, but potentially giving rise to all kinds of irrelevant speculations about the number and whereabouts of her children, whether they might have succeeded Macbeth, and so on. Knights argues, in what we may loosely call New Critical terms that this play, indeed any Shakespeare play, is more profitably approached as a dramatic poem than as either a portrait of life or a versified novel. This squared readily with the 1930s concentration on the recurrent themes and images in Shakespeare's plays, represented notably in the works of G. Wilson Knight (*b.*1897) whose essay, 'The Milk of Concord: an Essay on Life Themes in *Macbeth*' appeared in *The Imperial Theme* (1931) (his seminal work was *The Wheel of Fire*, 1930), and of Caroline Spurgeon (1869–1942), particularly in her *Shakespeare's Imagery and What It Tells Us* (1935). 'The Milk of Concord' characteristically begins with a quotation from the Lord's Prayer and proceeds to point out the major themes embodied in the play's imagery: fear, honour, feasting, darkness, evil, nature and 'life born out of death'; these are traced not merely for their own sake but as the basis of what can only be described as an inspirational reading of the play, laying emphasis on the way that 'life themes' emerge from the horror and darkness of the action. Caroline Spurgeon uses a very similar technique to very different ends; she argues that

> the imagery in *Macbeth* appears to me to be more rich and varied, more highly imaginative, more unapproachable by any other writer, than that of any other single play. It is particularly so, I think, in the continuous use made of the simplest, humblest, everyday things, drawn from the daily life in a small house, as a vehicle for sublime poetry.

(Compare this with Johnson's *Rambler* essay, quoted above.) She points particularly to the image of loose and ill-fitting garments associated with Macbeth's usurpation, and then to 'the symbolism that light stands for life, virtue, goodness; and darkness for evil and death'. These insights have been picked up and developed in different ways by many subsequent critics, notably Cleanth Brooks, whose essay, 'The Naked Babe and the Cloak of Manliness', appeared in his classic New Criticism volume, *The Well-Wrought Urn* (1947), and John Holloway (*b*.1920), whose chapter on Macbeth in *The School of Night* (1961) links the imagery of the ill-fitting clothes with the idea of Macbeth as a grotesque Lord of Misrule. Studies of the imagery of Shakespeare's plays sometimes see it as a key to his unconscious habits and sympathies (Caroline Spurgeon herself suggests that 'he, to some extent unconsciously, "gives himself away"'), sometimes merely as a contribution to the 'mood' of the play, sometimes as proof of the plays' imaginative unity (pursuing Coleridge's insights). They have even been used (for example, by E. A. Armstrong in *Shakespeare's Imagination*, 1946) to 'prove' that the Porter scene, rejected by Coleridge and others, really is by Shakespeare, since it reiterates many of the significant themes of the play – drink, sleep, darkness, damnation – albeit in a different mode from the rest of the play. As with so many critical approaches, the methodology may seem objective enough – pointing to themes and images that are indisputably present in the work; but what a critic makes of these insights is entirely another matter.

Parallel to the interest in the play's themes and images there grew up an interest in the play's philosophical content and context: is it essentially a Christian play (a question carefully avoided by Bradley and others because it might be thought that Christianity was incompatible with real tragedy)? Is it more medieval in emphasis (a morality play, in effect) or more Renaissance (essentially in sympathy with voyages into new intellectual and moral regions, whatever the cost)? Key works in this context are W. C. Curry, *Shakespeare's Philosophical Patterns* (1937) and V. K. Whitaker's *Shakespeare's Use of Learning* (1953), both of which stress the influence of medieval scholastic philosophy and theology on Shakespeare's thinking. R. Walker's *The Time is Free* (1949) and G. R. Elliott's *Dramatic Providence in 'Macbeth': A Study of Shakespeare's Tragic Theme of Humanity and Grace* (1958) are both thorough-going Christian readings of the play. There is a less doctrinaire account of the play's 'temper . . . the spirit in which it appears to have been conceived' in Wilbur Sanders's essay, 'The "Strong Pessimism" of *Macbeth*', incorporated in his *The Dramatist and the Received Idea* (1968). An off-shoot of this interest in the play's philosophical concerns has been an exploration of the possibility that it was written with the intention of indulging King James's particular interests; see, for example, H. N. Paul, *The Royal Play of Macbeth* (1950) and J. H. Jack's article, 'Macbeth, King James and the Bible' (*Journal of English Literary History*, 1955).

In reaction to the pervasive modern concentration on the play as a dramatic poem or as a philosophical tract, there has developed a school of thought which insists on it as primarily a text for the theatre. So, for example, *Macbeth* is one of the plays treated in the actor, dramatist and producer Harley Granville-Barker's (1877–1946) exhaustive *Prefaces to Shakespeare* (published in four series, 1927, 1930, 1937, 1945), which give detailed, scene-by-scene accounts of the problems involved in staging the plays. This approach inevitably lends strong interest to the ways in which major actors and directors have handled the play in production; the parts of Macbeth and Lady Macbeth have been played by virtually all the great actors and actresses from Richard Burbage, Shakespeare's principal tragic actor, to the present day. This play has, however, notoriously acquired a superstitious reputation for bad luck and many theatrical people will only refer to it by circumlocutions such as 'that Scottish play'; productions have been staged in which the final scene was never rehearsed. The eighteenth-century actor John Philip Kemble (1757–1823) published his thoughts on the play in *Macbeth Reconsidered* (1786) and his sister, the great Sarah Siddons (1755–1831), left some 'Remarks on the Character of Lady Macbeth', which were printed in Campbell's *Life of Mrs Siddons* (1834). These and later testaments in the same vein add up to what we might call an 'alternative criticism' of the play, to which modern scholars have been adding by their efforts in theatrical archaeology, as for example in G. W. Stone's essay on 'Garrick's Handling of *Macbeth*' (*Studies in Philology*, 1941). Much of this material has been collected and analysed in Marvin Rosenberg's *The Masks of Macbeth* (1978), as part of his major study of the stage-history of Shakespeare's plays. Latterly, a new dimension has been added to this field of study by the advent of film; *Macbeth* has been filmed memorably by Orson Welles (*b*.1915) (1948), Roman Polanski (*b*.1933) (1971) and, in an adaptation to Japanese samurai conventions, by Akira Kurosawa (*b*.1910) (as *Throne of Blood*, 1957). Any adaptation to a different medium poses questions of critical interpretation and appreciation; the viability of Shakespeare's plays as material for film and television is thus an issue of significance in the modern critical debate, not least since far more people are likely to see such versions than stage productions.

Finally, no one interested in *Macbeth* should ignore the American humorist James Thurber's (1894–1961) delightful *jeu d'esprit*, 'The *Macbeth* Murder Mystery', reprinted in *The Thurber Carnival* (1945). Its examination of the play as a detective story (the Macbeths could not have killed Duncan, since that is too obvious . . . .) is in no sense serious criticism, but its playful perversity may stand as a useful corrective to many ill-conceived and self-important approaches to this and other great works.

Macbeth has never enjoyed the near-universal reverence granted to *Hamlet* or the respect bordering on worship currently accorded to *King Lear*, but its greatness is assured. Individual critics have worried about the Porter scene, about the quality of the text as it has survived (it is very short and has obvious deficiencies) and other matters, but there is near-unanimity about the play's quality, whatever approach is applied. This is surely a measure of greatness – though we must beware of bestowing *automatic* praise even on Shakespeare, whose works have increasingly taken on a mythic status, as a part of our folk-culture which is all too often merely accepted and not thought about. *Macbeth* itself has become almost certainly the most widely studied of Shakespeare's tragedies at high-school level for reasons which are only marginally related to the critical history we have just outlined: it is short, its plot is relatively easy to follow and sex scarcely rears its ugly head to embarrass teachers. Unspoken assumptions such as these often count as much in criticism as spoken ones. It is unfortunately the case that one useful function of published criticism is often to jolt us out of the complacent and half-formed attitudes to literature with which too many of us are indoctrinated at school.

Songs and Sonets by John Donne

Donne's poems, originally written to be read only by friends and acquaintances, were not published until 1633, after his death, and his love poetry was not collected together as *Songs and Sonets* until 1635 – which means that we have neither Donne's own sanction for the collection nor any certainty as to the accuracy of the texts. We do know, however, that during his own lifetime his poems were highly respected by those like Ben Jonson, who called Donne 'the first poet in the world, for some things' (*Conversations with William Drummond*, 1618–19). But

Jonson also affirmed 'Donne to have written all his best pieces ere he was twenty-five years old', which may imply that he preferred the Donne of the Elegies and Satires, generally written by that time, to the Donne of the love poems, some of which were certainly later than the 1597 implied in the comment. Jonson also made two further remarks to Drummond* that have echoed through later critical debates: 'that Donne, for not keeping of accent, deserved hanging' and 'that Donne himself, for not being understood, would perish'. It was not only later ages which found Donne's metrical experiments and his obscurity perplexing.

Donne's reputation as a poet, which we may distinguish from his reputation as a preacher, much the stronger in the century after his death, was secure as long as his influence was acknowledged by practising poets; Thomas Carew (c.1598–c.1639), for example, wrote an 'Elegy' on Donne's death, concluding with a famous epitaph that pays homage to him both as a poet and as a priest:

Here lies a King, that rul'd as he thought fit
The universal monarchy of wit;
Here lie two flamens, and both those, the best,
Apollo's first, at last, the true God's priest.

But tastes changed rapidly after the Civil War. The biographer and essayist Isaac Walton (1593–1683) wrote a *Life* of Donne, originally attached to a 1640 edition of his sermons; but it is more the life of the priest than the poet. In 1655, Walton quotes the poem, 'The Bait', an adaptation of Marlowe's 'The Passionate Shepherd to His Love', in *The Compleat Angler*, with the comment that it was 'made to show the world that [Dr Donne] could make soft and smooth verses, when he thought fit and worth his labour' – which implies that his more normal, 'rugged' style was out of favour by that time. The attack is taken up again by Dryden, who complained that

he affects the metaphysics, not only in his satires, but in his amorous verses, where nature only should reign; and perplexes the minds of the fair sex with nice [over-fine] speculations of philosophy, when he should engage their hearts and entertain them with the softnesses of love (*A Discourse Concerning the Original and Progress of Satire*, 1693).

This passage may have given rise to the label, 'the Metaphysical poets' which has since been adopted almost universally in connection with Donne and various other poets of the first half of the seventeenth century; there is no evidence that he or they ever used it themselves – or that they would have acknowledged the similarities between their works assumed by people who use the label. Jonson, for example, not usually

*William Drummond of Hawthornden (1585-1649), a Scots poet.

described as a 'Metaphysical poet', felt that his writing had something in common with that of Donne; labels can easily obscure as much as they clarify.

Dryden's objections to Donne's 'metaphysical' style and complexity set the tone for the standard eighteenth-century view of Donne having 'a redundancy of wit', his poetry 'nothing but a continued heap of riddles', all of which was memorably summarised in Dr Johnson's *Life of Cowley* (1779), though it should be remembered that Johnson was really castigating the extravagances of Donne's imitators rather than Donne himself:

> The metaphysical poets were men of learning, and to show their learning was their whole endeavour; but, unluckily resolving to show it in rhyme, instead of writing poetry, they only wrote verses . . . . If . . . that be considered as Wit, which is at once natural and new, that which, though not obvious, is, upon its first production, acknowledged to be just; if it be that, which he that never found it, wonders how he missed; to wit of this kind the metaphysical poets have seldom risen. Their thoughts are often new, but seldom natural; they are not obvious, but neither are they just; and the reader, far from wondering that he missed them, wonders by what perverseness of industry they were ever found. But Wit . . . may be more rigorously and philosophically considered as . . . a combination of dissimilar images, or discovery of occult resemblances in things apparently unlike. Of wit, thus defined, they have more than enough. The most heterogeneous ideas are yoked by violence together; nature and art are ransacked for illustrations, comparisons, and allusions; their learning instructs, and their subtilty surprises; but the reader commonly thinks his improvement dearly bought, and though he sometimes admires is seldom pleased.

This famous passage illustrates an important truth about criticism in general. If we disagree with Johnson's view of Donne and the Metaphysical poets, we do so because of his *appreciation*, his valuation of them, not of his *understanding*, his description; surely he is correct in observing that their wit is not the wit of Pope and the eighteenth century, and in describing the way in which 'the most heterogeneous ideas are yoked by violence together' in their poetry. Where we are likely to part company with Johnson is in his unquestioning preference for eighteenth-century standards of wit and his unsubstantiated assertion that the Metaphysicals were only really 'showing off' their learning, implying that their poetry is not fundamentally serious. We disagree, in short, with his appreciation of their poetry, not with his reading of it. It would be difficult to find a passage which better demonstrates the fact that criticism chronicles *taste* as much as it does *insight*, or that the best criticism retains a validity of observation and interpretation even when the taste it champions is no longer shared.

Something of a change of taste is signalled in Coleridge's evident enthusiasm for Donne, in spite of what he saw as his 'detestable' faults. This is registered in marginal notes, such as 'Wonder-exciting vigour, intenseness and peculiarity of thought, using at will the almost boundless stores of a capacious memory, and exercised on subjects, where we have no right to expect it – this is the wit of Donne!' and also in the little poem, 'On Donne's Poetry':

> With Donne, whose muse on dromedary trots,
> Wreathe iron pokers into true-love knots;
> Rhyme's sturdy cripple, fancy's maze and clue,
> Wit's forge and fire-blast, meaning's press and screw.

But Coleridge left no major statement on Donne and, while we know that his poetry was read by authors such as Tennyson* and George Eliot, the nineteenth century as a whole found his poetry lacking in the things it valued. Hazlitt's comment – that Donne is 'led, particularly in his satires, to tell disagreeable truths in as disagreeable a way as possible, or to convey a pleasing and affecting thought (of which there are many to be found in his other writings) by the harshest means, and with the most painful effort' – is typical of the age's perplexity that a man who was still widely respected for his sermons should be so 'disagreeable' as a poet.

It is not until the end of the century – after Darwin and his disciples had delivered a sharp blow to Victorian complacency – that a real current of enthusiasm for Donne's poetry begins to emerge. George Saintsbury's (1845–1933) introduction to E. K. Chambers's 1896 edition of *The Poems of John Donne* marks the change:

> in Donne's case the yea-nay fashion of censorship which is necessary and desirable in the case of others is quite superfluous. His faults are so gross, so open, so palpable, that they hardly require the usual amount of critical comment and condemnation . . . . But for those who have experienced, or who at least understand, the ups-and-downs, the ins-and-outs of human temperament, the alternations not merely of passion and satiety, but of passion and laughter, of passion and melancholy reflection, of passion earthly enough and spiritual rapture almost heavenly, there is no poet and hardly any writer like Donne.

Donne's stylistic faults, which are still deemed to be 'gross' and 'palpable', are to be overlooked because the content of his verse, its

---

*Alfred, Lord Tennyson (1809–92), the major Victorian poet, author of *In Memoriam* (1850).

delineation of passion and spirituality, is so compelling – we might almost say 'realistic'. It is surely not coincidental that this was written only a year after Hardy's *Jude the Obscure* (1896) had caused such heated controversy with its frank handling of passion and religious scepticism.

A real watershed in the appreciation of Donne came with the edition of *The Poems of John Donne* made by H. J. C. Grierson (1866–1960), Saintsbury's successor at the University of Edinburgh, for the Oxford University Press in 1912. This was notable partly because it represented the first major scholarly effort to establish exactly what Donne had written both in the sense of which poems were really by him, and which versions of the many that have survived in manuscript most closely correspond to what he actually wrote, but also partly because Grierson's notes and introduction helped to 'place' Donne's poetry in the artistic and intellectual movements of its time, and in so doing largely explained away his 'gross' and 'palpable' faults. It was a classic demonstration of how scholarship and criticism could go hand-in-hand:

> Donne's love-poetry is a very complex phenomenon, but the two dominant strains in it are just these: the strain of dialectic, subtle play of argument and wit, erudite and fantastic; and the strain of vivid realism, the record of a passion which is not ideal nor conventional, neither recollected in tranquillity nor a pure product of literary fashion, but love as an actual, immediate experience in all its moods, gay and angry, scornful and rapturous with joy, touched with tenderness and darkened with sorrow – though these last two moods, the commonest in love-poetry, are with Donne the rarest. The first of these strains comes to Donne from the Middle Ages, the dialectic of the Schools, which passed into mediaeval love-poetry almost from its inception; the second is the expression of the new temper of the Renaissance as Donne had assimilated it in Latin countries (Introduction).

Paradoxically, the more firmly Donne was 'placed' in his time, the more lively and attractive he seemed to be; the testimony of poets as different as W. B. Yeats and Rupert Brooke (1887–1915) makes it clear that Grierson's edition re-established Donne as a truly major poet, for the first time, really, since his death, one whom that generation was able to look to almost as a contemporary.

If Grierson may be said to have resurrected Donne, Eliot may be said to have deified him. Donne became for Eliot and for many of his disciples the image of the true poet, as Keats had been for the Pre-Raphaelites and many people of the previous generation; many of the reasons for this are explained in an influential passage in an essay on 'The Metaphysical Poets' (1921):

A thought to Donne was an experience; it modified his sensibility. When a poet's mind is perfectly equipped for its work, it is constantly amalgamating disparate experience; the ordinary man's experience is chaotic, irregular, fragmentary. The latter falls in love, or reads Spinoza, and these two experiences have nothing to do with each other, or with the noise of the typewriter or the smell of cooking; in the mind of the poet these experiences are always forming new wholes. We may express the difference by the following theory: The poets of the seventeenth century, the successors of the dramatists of the sixteenth, possessed a mechanism of sensibility which could devour any kind of experience. They are simple, artificial, difficult, or fantastic, as their predecessors were . . . . In the seventeenth century a dissociation of sensibility set in, from which we have never recovered.

In retrospect we may feel that this tells us as much about Eliot, and the kind of poetry he was trying to write himself, as it does about Donne, but at the time it conferred almost canonical status on the 'Songs and Sonets'. Donne's love poems became exemplary models of what poetry should be for the New Critics; the qualities Eliot admired readily translated into the kinds of ambiguity, irony, paradox and verbal tension they were looking for. Chapter 4 of Empson's *Seven Types of Ambiguity* is devoted to Donne; he stands at the head of 'The Line of Wit' in Leavis's *Revaluation*; and he provides the title and a major chapter in Brooks's *The Well-Wrought Urn*.

On the whole, however, recent criticism of Donne has adopted a more sober tone – some of it positively antagonistic to what it sees as the exaggerated claims made for his poetry by Eliot and the New Critics, and some of it concerned further to explore his philosophy and his medieval/Renaissance context in ways which, whether intentionally or not, have diminished our sense both of his originality and of his being somehow our 'contemporary'. A key essay in the first category is C. S. Lewis's (1898–1963) 'Donne and Love Poetry in the Seventeenth Century' (in *Seventeenth Century Studies Presented to Sir Herbert Grierson*, ed. J. D. Wilson, 1938), which argues coolly that 'it is not impossible to see why Donne's poetry should be overrated in the twentieth century and underrated in the eighteenth century', asserts that 'paradoxical as it may seem, Donne's poetry is too simple to satisfy. Its complexity is all on the surface – an intellectual and fully-conscious complexity that we soon come to the end of', and puts down his current popularity to 'the mere frenzy of anti-romanticism'. Like a number of other writers, Lewis was convinced that the sheer range of attitudes reflected in Donne's love poetry adds up to an immature *playing* with thoughts and emotions rather than philosophical seriousness. Among more sympathetic studies of his 'philosophical method' have been J. B. Leishman's *The Monarch of Wit* (1951), Arnold Stein's *John Donne's*

Lyrics: the Eloquence of Action (1962) and Louis Martz's *The Wit of Love* (1969). Interesting parallel studies in Donne's indebtedness to Renaissance sources are Helen Gardner's 'The Argument about "The Ecstasy"' (in *Elizabethan and Jacobean Studies*, ed. H. Davis and H. Gardner, 1959) and A. J. Smith's 'The Metaphysic of Love' (*Review of English Studies*, New Series, IX, November 1958) – both concentrating on 'The Ecstasy', a poem which features more often than any other in arguments over Donne's originality, philosophic seriousness and poetic sincerity. It was an indication of the polarisation that had occurred in the criticism of Donne's love poetry – between those who insisted that he was a truly original and serious poet and those who emphasised the derivative nature of his style and the shallowness of his 'philosophy' – that Patrick Crutwell's essay (in *Metaphysical Poetry*, ed. M. Bradbury and D. Palmer, 1970) should be entitled: 'The Love Poetry of John Donne: Pedantique Weeds or Fresh Invention'.

The Donne who spoke so directly to the first readers of Grierson's edition was in danger of being swallowed up in a tide of 'philosophical' exegesis and unending debts to earlier writers, but a new interest in Donne the man has arisen and helped to put these academic studies, to some extent, in perspective. One symptom of this was Helen Gardner's decision in her edition of *The Songs and Sonets* (Oxford, 1965) to abandon the usual arrangement of the poems, based on the earliest printed text (but certainly not sanctioned by Donne or to any apparent design), and replace it with a sharp division: poems deemed to belong to the period before his marriage in 1601 and those deemed to belong to the period after it. The difficulty is that few of the poems can be dated with any certainty and so the division is largely based on subjective opinion: flippant, cynical and satirical items are generally consigned to the earlier period; works showing greater 'philosophical' interest and metrical complexity to the latter. This arrangement has not met with general favour, but the impulse behind it – to rediscover Donne as a living individual, whose poems in some way reflect the experience of a vital personality, albeit one conditioned by the cultural climate of his time – has remained strong, and was given a boost by the appearance of R. C. Bald's definitive biography, *John Donne: A Life* (1970). The most challenging attempt to read Donne's poetry in the context of his life and personality has been John Carey's *John Donne: Life, Mind and Art* (1981), which makes a sophisticated attempt to cut across conventional limits of biography and literary history in order to illuminate the writing; the danger of such an approach is the risk of producing a self-defining and self-selecting *version* of biography, history and poetry which finally illuminates nothing more than itself. But at its best such an approach may place the poetry vividly in perspective. It may be one of Donne's continuing claims to eminence that he is the earliest poet in the language of whose life we know sufficient to make such an approach viable. In that sense, whether we see him at the head of some 'line of wit' or not, he is likely to remain the earliest 'modern' English poet.

Donne's reputation as one of the major figures of English literature seems assured, though he has lost the special eminence he was accorded in the early part of the century. Poets such as Spenser and Milton, who tended to suffer by comparison with Donne's particular merits, have re-asserted themselves with more recent interest in myth, allegory and narrative theory – areas of study in which Donne scarcely figures. He is of some interest to proponents of stylistics (see, for example, G. Leech, *A Linguistic Guide to English Poetry*, 1969), but he seems less likely to be a major figure for structuralists. Donne remains a favourite in classrooms, albeit perhaps only for a limited number of poems – not even all the 'Songs and Sonets'; his dramatic and unconventional description of feelings and situations to which most people readily relate usually finds favour. The challenge here is to make students aware of his profound debts to neo-Platonic and Scholastic philosophy, his involvement in the obscure theological controversies of his day, and so dispel any illusions that he is a naive poet, *merely* chronicling personal experiences, while at the same time retaining a sense of his freshness and originality.

Few critical reputations have fluctuated quite so dramatically as Donne's, though that of one of his supposed followers, the poet, satirist and politician Andrew Marvell (1621–78), has run a roughly parallel course. The reasons for this should be of interest in themselves and should cause us to reflect on just how firmly grounded our current estimates of major figures are. At the same time, Donne is the kind of writer who, for a number of reasons, tends to attract a good deal of naive and ill-informed attention: what did he really think about women? was he sincere in becoming a priest? These are not questions that literary criticism asks. Literary criticism is finally about understanding and appreciating what a man writes – not understanding and appreciating the man himself – though the latter may help us to the former, if we keep the distinction clearly in mind. The study of Donne, more than of most poets, presents us graphically with this distinction. Anyone in doubt about whether to study literature at university would be well advised to consider this question.

Great Expectations by Charles Dickens

The initial reception of *Great Expectations* has to be seen in the context of the trough into which Dickens's reputation had fallen in the late 1850s; this 'reputation', though ultimately based on the sales of

Dickens's novels, was to a large extent shaped and moulded, troughs and all, by the literary reviewers of the time. After early triumphant success, in the period from *The Pickwick Papers* (1836–7) to *David Copperfield* (1849–50), Dickens steadily lost his popular appeal as his later novels such as *Bleak House, Little Dorrit* and *A Tale of Two Cities* reflected an increasingly sombre mood. A number of the early reviewers of *Great Expectations* hailed it as a return to the old Dickens. E. S. Dallas in *The Times*,17 October 1861, for example, rejoiced that

> Mr Dickens has good-naturedly granted to the hosts of his readers the desire of their hearts . . . . Without calling upon his readers for any alarming sacrifices, Mr. Dickens has in the present work given us more of his earlier fancies than we have had for years. *Great Expectations* is not, indeed, his best work, but it is to be ranked among his happiest. There is that flowing humour in it which disarms criticism, and which is all the more enjoyable because it defies criticism.

H. F. Chorley in *The Athenaeum*, 13 July 1861, hailed *Great Expectations* as 'the imaginative book of the year':

> Trying Mr. Dickens by himself, we find in this his last tale as much force as in the most forcible portions of *Oliver Twist*, as much delicacy as in the most delicate passages of *David Copperfield*, as much quaint humour as in *Pickwick*. In short . . . this is the creation of a great artist in his prime.

He tried to forestall some possible objections – 'There are those who will say that Miss Havisham's strange mad life is overdrawn; but such have not been conversant with the freaks and eccentricities which a haughty spirit in agony can assume' – but failed to convince a number of people, including the anonymous writer in the *Saturday Review*, 20 July 1861:

> Mr. Dickens has always had one great fault . . . that of exaggerating one particular set of facts, a comic side in a character, or a comic turn of expression, until all reality fades away . . . . Miss Havisham is one of Mr. Dickens's regular pieces of melodramatic exaggeration.

This writer does, however, concede that 'Mr. Dickens may be reasonably proud of these volumes. After the long series of his varied works – after passing under the cloud of *Little Dorrit* and *Bleak House* – he has written a story that is new, original, powerful and very entertaining'; he particularly approves of the fact that 'there are passages and conceptions in it which indicate a more profound study of the general nature of human character than Mr. Dickens usually betrays.' Only Mrs Margaret Oliphant, writing later than most in *Blackwood's Magazine* (May, 1862), was really disappointed:

> So far as *Great Expectations* is a sensation novel, it occupies itself with
> incidents all but impossible, and in themselves strange, dangerous,
> and exciting; but so far as it is one of the series of Mr. Dickens' work, it
> is feeble, fatigued, and colourless. One feels that he must have got
> tired of it as the work went on . . . .

One of the crosses that a modern writer such as Dickens (unlike
Shakespeare and Donne) has to bear is the reception of his published
works by reviewers like this – all honourable people, no doubt, but their
prejudices and preconceptions invariably seem to figure more
prominently than we would expect in more formal criticism. But one
striking feature of the reception given to *Great Expectations* is the
number of themes and issues it raised which have echoed down in the
criticism of the novel to this day, however much opinions may have
shifted on some of these matters. Firstly, there is the determination to
see the novel as part of Dickens's unfolding career rather than as an
individual work; this is coupled with a favourite vice of reviewers, and
perhaps of readers more generally, which is a wish that, once an author
has done something well, he will go on doing the same thing for the rest
of his life – the tendency to castigate *Great Expectations* for not being
The Pickwick Papers or *Oliver Twist* is quite evident. There is also the
question of Dickens's 'melodramatic exaggeration' of characters;
opinion on this seems to divide between those who do not see it as a
problem as long as it contributes to the 'flowing humour' which they
value so much in Dickens, and those who are exercised about how
'realistic' such an approach may be. On the one hand there are those
who insist that Miss Havisham is a truthful depiction of a 'haughty
spirit', and on the other those who insist that she is merely an example of
a character trait being exaggerated 'until all reality fades away'. The
fundamental assumption is common to all, however, that *realism* is the
name of the game – whatever differences there may be as to whether it is
achieved or not, and whatever allowances are made for 'humour'. This
was commonly the case of novel criticism at this time.

A number of the early reviewers also pointed to the obvious fact that
Great Expectations follows the example of *David Copperfield* in being
narrated as a first-person autobiography, with extensive childhood
scenes. They seemed to find that the comic vitality of the earlier work
pervaded the later one. They were followed in this by Dickens's friend
and biographer, John Forster (1812–76):

> It may be doubted if Dickens could better have established his right to
> the front rank among novelists claimed for him, than by the ease and
> mastery with which, in these two books of *Copperfield* and *Great
> Expectations*, he kept perfectly distinct the two stories of a boy's
> childhood, both told in the form of autobiography . . . . The

characters generally afford the same evidence ... that Dickens's humour, not less than his creative power, was at its best in [*Great Expectations*] (*The Life of Charles Dickens*, 1874).

This same book revealed for the first time that the ending of the novel as published, in which we are all but promised that Pip and Estella will marry, with reasonable happiness, was not the one Dickens originally conceived, which was altogether more disenchanted, and that the change was made at the instigation of his friend and fellow-novelist, Bulwer-Lytton (1803–73). Forster quotes a letter in which Dickens mentions (cynically? flippantly?) that 'I have put in as pretty a little piece of writing as I could, and I have no doubt the story will be more acceptable through the alteration', and then comments himself: 'This turned out to be the case; but the first ending nevertheless seems to be more consistent with the drift, as well as natural working out, of the tale.' This has remained a fruitful source of critical controversy ever since; it perfectly focuses such issues as artistic integrity, the special problems of writing for periodical publication and whether there really can be such a thing as the 'natural working out' of a piece of creative fiction. See, for example, Martin Meisel, 'The Ending of *Great Expectations*', *Essays in Criticism*, 15 July 1965.

On the whole, however, *Great Expectations* does not figure very prominently in the criticism that appeared in the years after Dickens's death. The biographer and critic G. H. Lewes (1817–78) does not mention it in his retrospective essay for the *Fortnightly Review*, 'Dickens in Relation to Criticism' (1872); the novelist George Gissing ‑(1857–1903) calls it 'that rich little book' but has relatively little to say about it in his *Charles Dickens* (1898). Similarly, the essayist, novelist and poet G. K. Chesterton (1874–1936) acknowledged that it was a 'fine story ... told with a consistency and quietude of individuality which is rare in Dickens'. By this he seems to mean that the first-person narrative subdued what he saw as the excesses of Dickens's usual style, but he shared the taste of Dickens's contemporaries for the comedy of the earlier novels and regretted 'the road of a heavier reality' which Dickens had travelled in this and other late works. In acknowledging the novel's moral and psychological power, he concedes that 'all this is very strong and wholesome; but it is still a little stern' and makes it clear that he approves of 'the robust romanticism of Bulwer-Lytton' which brought about the lighter ending' (*Charles Dickens*, 1906). Chesterton is aware that 'realism', 'the road to a heavier reality', is now a loaded term – novels can no longer simply be judged on subjective impressions of their 'lifelikeness'. The novelist and essayist E. M. Forster (1879–1970) addresses this question generally in his characteristically understated *Aspects of the Novel* (1927) and draws on *Great Expectations* for a number of examples; he compares the passage describing Mrs Gargery's funeral with a passage from the novelist H. G. Wells (1866–1946):

[The novelists] are, both, humorists and visualizers who get over an effect by cataloguing details and whisking the page over irritably. They are generous-minded; they hate shams and enjoy being indignant about them; they are valuable social reformers; they have no notion of confining books to a library shelf. Sometimes the lively surface of their prose scratches like a cheap gramophone record, a certain poorness of quality appears, and the face of the author draws rather too near to that of the reader.

Dickens is implicitly being contrasted with more discreet and self-effacing authors such as Jane Austen and Henry James; the inference is that their novels are 'art' while those of Dickens, whatever other virtues they have, are scarcely that. Forster makes the same point again in a famous passage about characterisation:

Dickens's people are nearly all flat (Pip and David Copperfield attempt roundness, but so diffidently that they seem more like bubbles than solids). Nearly every one can be summed up in a sentence, and yet there is this wonderful feeling of human depth . . . Those who dislike Dickens have an excellent case. He ought to be bad. He is actually one of our big writers, and his immense success with types suggests that there may be more in flatness than the severer critics admit.

Forster's distinction between 'flat' and 'rounded' characters is one that Dickens criticism has never really shaken off; it is nearly always advanced to his discredit, partly because – for all Forster's deference to Dickens as 'one of our big writers' – his terms of reference keep implying that the 'rounded' characters of such as Jane Austen and Henry James are the product of a more sophisticated art.

It was symptomatic of a radical change of taste that, in the Preface to a 1937 edition of *Great Expectations*, George Bernard Shaw focused upon, and applauded, what he saw as the novel's essential seriousness: 'It is too serious a book to be a trivially happy one. Its beginning is unhappy; its middle is unhappy; and the conventional happy ending is an outrage on it.' Two long essays that appeared shortly thereafter mark a watershed in Dickens criticism as a whole, and incidentally set the tone for the criticism of *Great Expectations* that was to come. The first was George Orwell's 'Charles Dickens' (1939), which he described as an attempt to answer the questions 'Why does anyone care about Dickens? Why do *I* care about Dickens?' The answer he came up with was to some extent an answer for the times, just before the outbreak of the Second

World War, and he summed it up in the idea of a 'face somewhere behind the page':

> It is the face of a man who is always fighting against something, but who fights in the open and is not frightened, the face of a man who is *generously angry* – in other words, of a nineteenth-century liberal, a free intelligence, a type hated with equal hatred by all the smelly little orthodoxies which are now contending for our souls.

This was an attempt to lay the ghost of Dickens as primarily the author of *Pickwick* and *A Christmas Carol*, to insist that, *despite his popularity*, he should still be taken seriously by intelligent people. One consequence of the insistence on the novel as an art form, largely instigated by Henry James and followed by critics like Forster, was that popularity became a suspect criterion: how could something be great art if it was also widely accessible? Orwell tries to counter this by insisting that the spirit and content of Dickens's novels matter more than their artistic 'form'. It was indicative of the climate of opinion that Orwell was protesting about, that there was no place for Dickens (except, rather oddly, for *Hard Times*) in F. R. Leavis's *The Great Tradition* (1948).

The second of the two long essays, and in many ways the more influential, was Edmund Wilson's 'Dickens: The Two Scrooges', published in *The Wound and The Bow* (1941). Wilson too starts from the assertion that Dickens 'has become for the English middle class so much one of the articles of their creed – a familiar joke, a favourite dish, a Christmas ritual – that it is difficult for British pundits to see in him the great artist and social critic that he was'. He sets out to counter this by stressing the element of social criticism in Dickens's novels and by emphasising the psychological gloom they so often reflect; the latter point in particular causes him to accord unusual prominence to the later novels, from *Bleak House* (1852–3) onwards. These are, for Wilson, and for virtually all the critics who follow him, the richest and most rewarding of Dickens's achievements; and *Great Expectations* emerges as a pivotal work:

> In *Great Expectations* we see Pip pass through a whole psychological cycle. At first, he is sympathetic, then by a more or less natural process he turns into something unsympathetic, then he becomes sympathetic again. Here the effects of both poverty and riches are seen from the inside in one person. This is for Dickens a great advance . . . .

Among the criticism of *Great Expectations* which may be said to follow directly from Wilson's essay are Dorothy Van Ghent's 'On *Great Expectations*' in *The English Novel: Form and Function* (1953); G. R. Strange's 'Expectations Well Lost: Dickens' Fable for his Time' (*College English*, XVI, October 1954); and Julian Moynahan's 'The

Hero's Guilt: the Case of *Great Expectations*' (*Essays in Criticism*, January 1960). All are connected in seeing the question of guilt as central to the novel's psychological, moral and artistic concerns. J. Hillis Miller (*Charles Dickens: the World of his Novels*, 1958) places Pip's guilt in a wider vision of the novel as a kind of re-working of *Paradise Lost*, while Barbara Hardy (*The Moral Art of Dickens*, 1970), focuses the whole question of moral accountability in the novel through its preoccupation with food: 'Food in *Great Expectations*, as in *Macbeth*, is part of the public order, and the meals testify to human need and dependence, and distinguish false ceremony from the ceremony of love.'

Recent criticism of *Great Expectations*, in short, is virtually unanimous in regarding it as a sombre and successful moral fable; there has been some occasional interest in the technical questions of the first-person narrative, periodical publication and the changed ending, but even these are generally measured in terms of their bearing on the overall moral tone/design of the novel. The revolution in taste that has taken place in the century or so since Dickens's death could hardly be more complete; it bears comparison with the shift in taste between Johnson – who looked to Shakespeare's comedies for the true artist – and Coleridge, who looked to the tragedies. Where Dickens's contemporaries looked for comedy, and apparently found it, we discover disturbing psychological concerns; where some of them – and later proponents of the 'art' of the novel – decried the caricature-style of the characterisation or rather feebly tried to defend it as 'realistic', most of us now calmly accept it as part of his complex, symbolically pointed style; where they yearned for him to keep repeating his exuberant early triumphs, we seem to be rather pleased, in a way, that his later years were riddled with doubts and anxieties – as titles such as *The Melancholy Man: a Study of Dickens's Novels* (John Lucas, 1970, 1980) and *The Violent Effigy: a Study of Dickens' Imagination* (John Carey, 1973) testify.

Like Shakespeare, Dickens seems to be sufficiently multi-faceted to have something significant to offer to each successive generation of critics. This may be one definition of greatness. It says something for Dickens's stature that so forceful a critic as F. R. Leavis, after all but dismissing him in *The Great Tradition*, felt obliged to recant and, with his wife, Q. D. Leavis, produced a full-scale study of the novels: *Dickens the Novelist* (1970). (The chapter on *Great Expectations* is in the characteristic imperative mode of his later years: 'How We Must Read *Great Expectations*'). The tradition of criticism of Dickens poses one question most acutely: how proper or useful is it to discuss individual texts in relation to a writer's other works or against the background of his supposed 'imaginative career'? Dickens seems especially to attract such criticism, with all the dangers it runs of prejudging or distorting a text in order to make it fit some preconceived pattern.

Once again, we should be aware that the popularity in the classroom of the text we have been considering is not entirely due to the qualities most frequently discussed in formal criticism. *Great Expectations* has the merit of being relatively short, unlike *Bleak House* (1852–3) or *Little Dorrit* (1855–7), the other masterpieces of Dickens's later career (which many critics would judge to be even finer works), and unlike Dickens's other fictional 'autobiography', *David Copperfield* (1849–50). It is also generally believed that young people find stories of growing up inherently interesting and 'relevant' to themselves: hence the frequent appearance of such texts as *Great Expectations*, James Joyce's *A Portrait of the Artist as a Young Man* (1914–15), D. H. Lawrence's *Sons and Lovers* (1913), J. D. Salinger's *The Catcher in the Rye* (1951) and Laurie Lee's *Cider with Rosie* (1959) on school syllabuses.

The books and essays mentioned in connection with the three texts we have been considering represent only a small fraction of the total available; the summary of the main critical trends which have confronted them is necessarily selective in the extreme. If you wish to know more about these – or any author or topic – you should start by consulting a suitable *bibliography*. The most useful general-purpose bibliography for literary critics is the *New Cambridge Bibliography of English Literature* (ed. G. Watson, 1969–77), though like all bibliographies this is now beginning to date, and if it is essential to know what has been published recently you should consult the most recent volumes of the *Annual Bibliography of English Literature* (1920–), issued by the Modern Humanities Research Association. There are also full-scale bibliographies individually devoted to most major authors; on those treated here, for example, you might consult: Stanley Wells (ed.), *Shakespeare: a Select Bibliographical Guide* (1973); J. R. Roberts, *John Donne: an Annotated Bibliography of Modern Criticism, 1912–1967* (1973); R. C. Churchill (ed.), *A Bibliography of Dickensian Criticism, 1836–1975* (1975). The crucial advantage that bibliographies offer is the opportunity to be *selective* in your reading of criticism, to start with a broad general view of what has been written and to home-in from there on what is most likely to be useful or of interest to you. A discussion of the staging of *Macbeth*, for example, will only be marginally useful if you are mainly interested in the imagery of the play; an essay on Donne's characteristic use of language will only help indirectly to an understanding of his philosophic concerns.

    At the end of Part 2 of this Handbook it was mentioned how intimidating it can be to be confronted with the whole mass of critical material available in modern libraries. A thoughtful use of biblio-graphies, or even the outline bibliographical material most critic books themselves contain, can make you its master rather than its sla

The main thing is to have a clear idea of what really interests you: with that in mind you will be able to make a deliberate and circumspect use of criticism as an adjunct and stimulus to your own thinking, rather than as a substitute for it. Having found something relevant, continue to treat it with caution and circumspection: what does it leave out? What does it miss that seems to you to matter, and why? Part 4 suggests ways in which you might set about formulating your own criticism when faced with a particular text or assignment, using existing criticism as an aid – but not as a crutch.

Part 4

The practice of criticism: a blueprint

No SINGLE TEXT CAN BE USED to demonstrate all the possibilities that a critic might explore. The one chosen here presents, for its size, more problems (or, should we say, openings) than most; but please regard these suggestions on how these problems might be approached as *typical of the methods* that might be employed on any text rather than as a definitive assessment of this text, or as an exhaustive account of all critical techniques. Where it has seemed useful to point to significant differences presented by other kinds of text, comments are printed in italics.

Let us imagine that you have been confronted by the following passage, having no idea who wrote it, where, or why, or when; and that you wish both to *understand* and *appreciate* it (perhaps this is required of you by a teacher):

> No longer mourn for me when I am dead,
> Than you shall hear the surly, sullen bell
> Give warning to the world that I am fled
> 4   From this vile world, with vilest worms to dwell:
> Nay, if you read this line, remember not,
> The hand that writ it; for I love you so,
> That I in your sweet thoughts would be forgot,
> 8   If thinking on me then should make you woe.
> O if (I say) you look upon this verse,
> When I (perhaps) compounded am with clay,
> Do not so much as my poor name rehearse;
> 12   But let your love even with my life decay.
>   Lest the wise world should look into your moan,
>   And mock you, with me, after I am gone.

It is not the intention here to offer a critical analysis of the passage, so much as to point you to ways that can enable you to do this for yourself. The way you finally choose should depend upon your own interests and preoccupations, unless you are doing this as an academic exercise, in which case the approach may be prescribed for you – for, let us hope, sound pedagogic reasons.

How would you begin to make sense of this passage, or to find something constructive to say about it? Firstly, have you read it through carefully, at least twice? This may not be practical with some longer texts (for example, a novel), but there is no real excuse for not taking such time and care with a shorter text – say, anything up to the length of a Shakespearean play. You may well be surprised how different the text seems on a second reading: what things stand out that you missed before? What features connect with others in ways you had not noticed before? Have you made notes about what you noticed on each read-through? Memory is notoriously unreliable, and you are only going to have the sketchiest notion of what you thought of the opening of, say, *Middlemarch* by the time you reach the end of it. Even for a short passage like this one, making notes of your impressions will help you to organise your thoughts. And have you tried reading it aloud? Reading aloud imposes a different kind of attention, forces a different kind of concentration, and so gives you a different perspective on the material. *No critical methodology, however sophisticated, will make up for careless or lazy reading.*

Our chosen text is not particularly obscure or difficult, even on a first reading. It makes no obvious allusions to specialist areas of knowledge, such as classical mythology, historical events or other works of literature. Nor does it use arcane or unusual vocabulary. Had it presented us with such problems, there would have been no alternative but to try to come to terms with them; this is only an extension of the requirement to read carefully.

Writers often make such allusions to alert us to themes and preoccupations in their works. When James Joyce calls a novel Ulysses *(Latin name for Odysseus, hero of Homer's* Odyssey*) or Aldous Huxley calls one* Brave New World *(a quotation from Shakespeare's* The Tempest*), we may assume that our understanding and appreciation of the work will be enhanced by a recognition of the allusion and its implications. Indeed, it may be impossible without such recognition: you are not going to make much of Yeats's poem, 'Leda and the Swan', without some knowledge of the Greek mythology to which it alludes. Of course, you may not always spot a quotation or be able to trace an allusion, but there is no excuse for not trying. Ideally, therefore, every literary critic should have access to the usual range of reference books: encyclopaedias, dictionaries of quotations and mythology,* The Oxford Companion to English Literature *and a dictionary which at least gives the etymology (derivation) of words as well as their meanings. These are the tools of his trade and he should not be too proud or lazy to use them. One word of caution, however: do not make the mistake of assuming that you have 'understood' a text simply because you have grasped something of its obscure allusions or arcane vocabulary. This is only a starting-point. What matters is what the* *author makes of such things. But such questions will not delay us with our chosen text.*

Our passage, in fact, is so straightforward that it would be relatively easy to offer a paraphrase of what it says, and this can always be a useful — exercise. The writer (for the sake of argument, let us assume him to be male) seems to anticipate his death and writes to some loved one (for the sake of argument, female) asking that she should not mourn after his death and burial; indeed, that she should not even remember him since he would not like his memory to cause distress; if she should read what he has written when he is long buried, let her resolutely forget his name and the love she had for him in case the world should enquire into her distress and mock her, as it mocks him, after he is dead.

In fact, such a paraphrase – another way of paying close attention – is always likely to reveal more problems than it solves. It certainly accentuates what we might call some of the passage's mysteries. Why is the writer dying? Must we assume that she knows already? Why is it a 'vile world' in line 4 and a 'wise world' in line 13? Is he only to be mocked after his death, or is he already being mocked? Why should he be mocked at all (for dying?), or she (for mourning? for having loved?)? We discover, in short, that although the words and ideas of the passage are not difficult in themselves, we do not apparently have all the information we need to make sense of them.

The business of reading is always essentially one of making sense of the information that a writer chooses to convey; and this is intimately tied up with the question of why that information matters at all. In this respect the detective novel is the epitome of all literature: the writer gives us such information as he pleases and then teases us into trying to make sense of it; he prides himself, in that instance, in giving us all the factual information we need – what remains in doubt until the final pages is how and why the information matters, how and why it makes sense. In that sense, all literature – Shakespeare's tragedies, Donne's love poetry, Dickens's novels, whatever – is a detective novel for the critic to solve. What makes the best literature so much more difficult to 'solve' than most detective novels is that it is not tied to a single comprehensible formula – it sets for itself the terms in which it makes sense. And in the passage we are considering, one of those terms is that some factual information is denied to us. We should not find this odd or unusual: what separates art from life is the selection of detail, the reduction of totality to what the artist considers significant, what he thinks matters.

One way forward from our apparent impasse is to ask whether any of the questions we might like answered are given *implicit* answers by the balance of such information as we do possess. Is there a balance of probabilities about how things make sense and why they matter? Can we deduce anything from the *tone* in which the existing information is conveyed? The evidence here seems to be ambiguous: the tone might be either one of breathless sincerity (the writer altruistically unconcerned about, even impatient for, his own death, but anxious that the loved one should not suffer in any way) or one of scathing sarcasm (the writer bitterly contemplating death because – he implies – the loved one does not care for him now, while he's alive, and is not likely to think about him when he is dead: let her beware the world's mockery, which he already feels, if she belatedly sheds crocodile tears).

Is there a single 'correct' tone in which to read the passage? How can we reconcile the multiplicity of possibilities? It is at this point that we might profitably turn to any one of the three modern critical approaches formulated to grapple with literary texts, if needs be, in a vacuum – the bare words on the page: New Criticism, stylistics and structuralism/ semiotics. (See the appropriate sections in Part 2.) Given our current limited knowledge of the passage's derivation, it is not possible, nor would it, necessarily, be desirable, to track down anything written from these points of view on our particular passage. What we want at this stage is something to sharpen and focus our own reading, a modus operandi, a coherent way of dealing with the text's complexities. So we might look for some basic exposition of the rationales behind the various approaches, with some examples of how they work in practice: for New Criticism, we might look to William Empson's Seven Types of Ambiguity or Cleanth Brooks's The Well-Wrought Urn; for stylistics, to Anne Cluysenaar's Introduction to Literary Stylistics (1976) or D. C. Freeman (ed.), Linguistics and Literary Style (1970); for structuralism, to Robert Scholes's Structuralism in Literature: An Introduction (1974) or Jonathan Culler's Structuralist Poetics: Structuralism, Linguistics and the Study of Literature (1975).

But these are not the only options open to us. So far no comment has been made on the fact that this passage is in verse (iambic pentameter, rhymed in three quatrains with a final couplet). It is, in fact, in one of the most distinctive and tightly organised of poetic forms, that of the sonnet. Attention has deliberately not been called to these features of the passage before now, since there is always a danger that recognising certain technical features or employing definitions will hinder a reading rather than help it. The lucky reader, who has read enough poetry to recognise a sonnet when he sees one, smiles and says, 'Oh, it's a sonnet' – as if that explains everything. Yet again, this is a beginning in our progress towards understanding and appreciation, not an ending; in itself, it explains nothing. It is, however, a beginning only available to someone whose reading in literature is sufficiently broad to enable him to distinguish between one literary form and another. It is, of course, possible to find abstract definitions of the sonnet – or the epic, or villanelle, or epistolary novel, or comedy of manners, or whatever – but there is no real substitute for a wide reading of literature if you wish to recognise such forms more or less instinctively, or if you wish to be able to appreciate how a particular use of such a form varies from other actual and possible uses.

Inasmuch as it is a sonnet, the chosen text is unrepresentative, since it is relatively rare to find pieces of literature so short which fall so obviously into a recognised generic form. But these comments have been cast in such a way that the general lessons would be equally valid if this were an extract from, say, an epic, a play or a novel. Notice, however, that in normal circumstances – when we are not asked to read a passage 'blind' – authors rely on the fact that many of our responses are conditioned by the knowledge or assumption that 'this is a novel' or 'this is a play'. Even in our chosen example, the author self-consciously admits that he is writing 'verse' (line 9) and does not pretend otherwise. Part of the business of reading is to acquire an equal self-consciousness, to be able to respond to the nuances such an intimacy allows.

For some readers it may be that the most impressive feature of the text is the way it accommodates itself to, or expresses itself through, the medium of verse (or the form of the sonnet). They will want to pursue these interests through general books on these topics, such as Winifred Nowottny, *The Language Poets Use* (1962), G. N. Leech, *A Linguistic Guide to English Poetry* (1969), G. S. Fraser, *Metre, Rhyme and Free Verse* (1970) and John Fuller, *The Sonnet* (1972).

There are, of course, equivalent introductory works on prose narrative and dramatic forms, but it would be redundant to list them here. It is at such points that bibliographies become invaluable – specifically here bibliographies organised on generic lines. See, for example, A. E. Dyson (ed.), The Novel: a Select Bibliographical Guide (1974) and S. Wells (ed.), English Drama, excluding Shakespeare: a Select Bibliographical Guide (1975). Also worth bearing in mind is the Critical Idiom series, published by Methuen, London, to which the books by Fraser and Fuller belong; useful introductions to topics themselves, these books also offer suggestions for further reading.

Any enquiry into the nature of verse will inevitably lead to a consideration of figurative or emotive language. In what sense can a bell be 'surly' or 'sullen' (line 2) or the world be 'wise' (line 13. See T. Hawkes, *Metaphor*, 1972). Likewise, any consideration of the sonnet form must take account of the poet's exploitation of the prescribed fourteen lines. In the traditional or Petrarchan form of the sonnet, as it was adapted from Italian originals into English in the sixteenth century, it was usual for a poet to expound a topic or problem in his first eight lines, and somehow develop or resolve it in his last six, employing one of a number of rhyme schemes linked to this pattern; but our sonnet is not like that. The first twelve lines all may be said to expound the same theme, each quatrain (four lines) adding to it; only the final couplet, a separate rhyming unit, may be said to offer a kind of resolution. This pattern is usually known as the Elizabethan sonnet. We may want here to ask in what way the Elizabethan sonnet pattern is appropriate or effective in this particular text.

Such effects are obviously easiest to identify and discuss in the limited confines of a sonnet, but there are analogies in more expansive forms of literature, particularly those in tightly defined genres. Milton's Paradise Lost *or Fielding's* Tom Jones, *for example, both derive many of their very different effects from the exploitation of the conventions of classical epics.* Hamlet *exploits the audience's expectations, based on earlier revenge tragedies.* Tristram Shandy *defies the conventions of first-person narrative, just as Agatha Christie breaks the 'rules' of detective fiction in* The Murder of Roger Ackroyd. *These are some of the issues to be considered when approaching literature via its genres.*

This takes us about as far as we can reasonably be expected to go (as far as some critics – for example, New Critics – would ever want to go), without knowing something of the sonnet's composition: specifically, who wrote it and approximately when. (The questions 'why?' and 'to whom?' pose separate problems which we shall consider in due course.) The sonnet is by Shakespeare; it is No. 71 of those of his sonnets which were first published in 1609. What difference does this information make? For one thing, it should certainly alert us to the near-certainty that the text as we have been given it is not as it was originally written or published – the spelling throughout is altogether too modern. We can readily check this by comparing our text with a facsimile of the 1609 text (few of us will have access to an original!) or with a modern text which faithfully reproduces the original. We will discover that both spelling (for example, 'vilest', for 'vildest' in line 4, 'moan' for 'mone' in line 13) and punctuation have, to some extent, been changed.

You may feel that they have not been changed very much, and that the sense or meaning has not been affected, but a crucial principle is at stake here (as anyone with any knowledge of structuralist criticism will appreciate): *any edition of a text is, to a greater or lesser degree, an interpretation of that text.* It follows that we need to be aware of this, to be prepared to take it into account in our own understanding and appreciation. Here is one example of how this could matter in this case: the commas in the last line ('And mock you, with me, after I am gone.') are not there in the original. What they do is to isolate and, as it were, emphasise the phrase 'with me'; in so doing they cut across a number of possible implications in the text. Is the 'wise world' liable to mock the lover *in addition to* the poet? Or is the poet *with* 'the wise world' in mocking the lover? Does the modernised punctuation appear to point to one reading in preference to the other? Should it? Does it make the

ambiguity of the final sentence more apparent than it need/should be?
And so on.

It is perhaps only in short works such as this that minor details of punctuation are liable to be so crucial. The ending of Keats's 'Ode on a Grecian Urn' is another famous example, where the punctuation leaves room for doubt whether the message of the urn is simply 'Beauty is truth, truth beauty' or the whole of the last two lines. But the general issue is much wider than a matter of punctuation and affects most of the texts which will be of interest to students of literature – certainly most of those published before the twentieth century. The point is: how close is the text that we have to what the author wrote, and what allowance do we need to make for the interference of a modern editor in our estimation of the work? Any modern text of a Shakespeare play, for example, emphasises the issue in extreme form: Shakespeare did not, apparently, prepare any plays for publication; several early versions of some plays exist, some more satisfactory than others, but none with a claim to be authoritative; all are, by modern standards, archaic in terms of spelling and punctuation; all are either lax in their indication of scene and act divisions, and in their provision of stage directions, or they follow conventions which are no longer intelligible to most readers. Virtually any modern text of a Shakespeare play is thus an educated compromise, merging the early alternatives into a single composite work and then rendering it in a form which will be intelligible to today's readers – at whatever cost in terms of spelling, punctuation, amendments of 'corrupt' text and general presentation.

Most critical activity takes all this for granted and gets on with the business of understanding and appreciation, using the most reputable modern text available; but a critic needs always to be aware, at least in general terms, of the kind of text he is using and the ways in which it is an interpretation of the work he is assessing. See, for example, the comments above on the Grierson and Gardner editions of Donne, pp. 91–3. We do not need, however, to go back to the time of Shakespeare or Donne for the nature of the text to pose problems for critics; many Victorian novels, such as Great Expectations, *were originally published in serial form and only later adapted for publication in book form. This may have a bearing on the way we read the text; it must certainly be borne in mind when comparing contemporary responses to such novels with our own. Any good edition will explain the principles upon which it is based, and will alert the reader (usually in foot- or end-notes) where a significant editorial decision has been made; the critic will be advised to pay attention to such details – it is yet another dimension to careful reading. The simple moral of all this is that it will always repay a critic to get – and use – a reputable text of whatever work he is interested in.*

Once we know who wrote a text (and when) the range of possible critical enquiry expands enormously. How legitimate or worthwhile some of these enquiries may be is debatable. On the whole we may say that, so long as an enquiry is pursued in the interests of understanding and appreciating a text or texts, it remains valid literary criticism. But when the text becomes only of secondary *importance – say, as evidence in some historical or sociological enquiry, or of the author's opinion on some matter – we have left the realms of literary criticism. Historians, sociologists and biographers (and other people such as linguisticians and psychologists) may, of course, have legitimate interests in literature, and the critic may often benefit indirectly from their insights; but he should beware of confusing his priorities with theirs.*

Having established the nature of our text, let us examine the further possibilities that are opened to us by our new knowledge. For one thing we can now say with confidence that we are dealing not only with a sonnet but specifically with one written in the Elizabethan era. This was the hey-day of the sonnet in England; certain themes and conventions were prevalent at the time which were less in evidence in later periods. We might consult a book on the topic, such as J. W. Lever, *The Elizabethan Love Sonnet* (1956). We might learn, for example, that the theme of the poet's dying is a common one in the sonnets of the period (usually because he has been scorned or deserted by the one he loves) and that there is a recurrent association of the themes of love and death, partly fostered by Elizabethan ideas about sex. This may cause us to rethink the nature of the 'sincerity' of the poem, or the literal truth of its statements, or indeed the whole context of thought and literary convention to which it belongs.

By the same token, our knowledge that a novel was Victorian or that a play was by an author – such as, for example, Samuel Beckett or Harold Pinter – who has been described as 'absurdist', might lead us to look further into the appropriate period, 'school' or 'movement'. We might find that such characters as a 'fallen' heroine, or a Byronic hero, or puzzled and puzzling tramps, were not so unexpected as we might have supposed. It is wise, indeed it is essential when consulting general books on Elizabethan sonnets or Victorian fiction or the Theatre of the Absurd, not to rely too heavily on a single work, since it will (inevitably, and with the best of intentions) be partial and biased; there is no such thing as an objective work of criticism, and there is much to be said for making your own comparison of your principal text(s) with other Elizabethan sonnets, Victorian novels and Absurdist plays, wherever possible.

Any work on Elizabethan sonnets would certainly confront us with the incontrovertible fact that it was commonplace to compile sonnets in extensive sequences, usually in such a way that a narrative of sorts can indistinctly be perceived through them. We might be encouraged, therefore, to consider this particular sonnet in the context of Shakespeare's sonnets as a whole, and especially of those printed in closest proximity with it. We would find, for example, that the theme of the poet's impending death and the anguished sense of his having been betrayed or abandoned by his lover recurs frequently around this point in the sequence. Should we allow this to affect our reading of this particular poem's ambiguities and complexities? A strict New Critic would say certainly not. But some generic and structuralist critics might argue that the *sequence* was the primary unit of meaning, rather than the individual sonnet, and so allow a broader definition of what was strictly relevant. The general issue here is the relationship between the constituent parts of a work and its total structure.

Shakespeare's sonnets are notoriously difficult in this respect, since the usual practice is to take the author's own intentions (either as stated or as implied in the latest edition that he had a hand in publishing) as defining 'the work', leaving it to critics to discern relationships between parts and the whole. But we have reason to suppose that Shakespeare did not wish to have his sonnets published (or, at least, publicly printed and distributed) at all. That is not to say, however, that he might not have arranged them in a sequence for the benefit of the original privileged readers (we know that there were 'sugared sonnets among his private friends' before 1598). On the other hand, even if he did, we cannot be sure that the published order actually represents Shakespeare's intentions. Some modern editors have been convinced that they can discern a more satisfactory sequence than the given one and have made adjustments accordingly – a clear case of the critical tail wagging the editorial dog.

Again, there is a general issue of principle to be considered. Some collections of poems are clearly intended by their authors to be read as complete works rather than as a number of parts – Ben Jonson's Epigrams, *for example, or George Herbert's (1593–1633)* The Temple, *or William Blake's (1757–1827)* Songs of Innocence and Experience. *In the case of Tennyson's* In Memoriam *it is doubtful whether we are dealing with a single poem or a collection of linked poems. These are in some ways exceptional works, but even in conventional narrative and dramatic works, where there is generally no mystery about the intended sequence, we may still usefully ask ourselves: why is this chapter/verse/canto/scene/book/ act here in this particular form? How does it connect with what went before and what comes after? In what ways does it contribute to the total structure or to the dominant themes?*

Occasionally, even a whole novel or a play may belong to what the author has designated as a deliberate sequence. There is nothing in English quite to match the French novelist Marcel Proust's (1871–1922) novel sequence, A la recherche du temps perdu, *but any number of novelists have written repeatedly about the same characters in such a way as to create sequences of sorts – for example, Anthony Trollope (1815–82) in the Barsetshire novels and the Palliser novels, John Galsworthy (1867–1933) in his* Forsyte Saga, *or Anthony Powell* (b. *1905) in his sequence* A Dance to the Music of Time. *In different ways we may find points of contact between some of Shakespeare's history plays, or Arnold Wesker's* (b. *1932) self-designated* Trilogy.

Even if there is no obvious larger structure or sequence to which a particular text belongs, it is common critical practice to give it one – in the sense that the works of any author are often deemed to form a composite whole. This may have nothing to do with what we do or do not know about the author's actual biography. In critical terms what matters is the way we may perceive certain themes, attitudes, approaches, conventions (or whatever) being repeated, adapted, developed, explored within an author's *corpus*. It is probably the case that a majority of critical books published start from the assumption that it will be useful to consider a writer's works – either in whole or in part – as linked products, manifesting certain technical or thematic preoccupations, which may abstractly be summarised as his 'art' or 'vision' (or perhaps 'philosophy'). One way of dealing with our sonnet may be to assess its place in the 'art' or 'vision' of the author as a whole.

It is difficult to conceive that a single sonnet can usefully be compared to a Shakespearean play since the scale and conventions are so disparate, but there is plenty of scope for examining, say, the themes of love and death as treated in the sonnets and in the romantic tragedies (*Romeo and Juliet, Othello, Troilus and Cressida* – not strictly a tragedy, but apt – *Antony and Cleopatra*); or the depiction of 'poetic lovers' in *Love's Labour's Lost* and *As You Like It* with their counterparts in the sonnets; or for exploring the peculiarly *dramatic* quality of the best sonnets – their capacity for implying real situations, clashes of personality and so on. In such ways we may place a small text in relation to the *corpus* as a whole.

The critical history of all three texts considered in Part 3 is littered with works dedicated to this principle. It is commonplace, for example, to 'place' Macbeth *in the middle of an argument over whether there is such a thing as Shakespearean tragedy (that is, a developing sub-genre with definable characteristics) or merely a number of tragedies by Shakespeare (that is, more notable for their differences than their similarities); it is equally commonplace to consider* Macbeth *as a more sympathetic re-working of other usurpation plots, such as those of* Richard III *and of Claudius in* Hamlet. *Similarly, critics never tire of explaining how alike in essentials are the Jack Donne of the* Songs and Sonets *and the Dr Donne of the Divine Poems and the Sermons. And, as we saw, the first instinct of contemporary reviewers was to compare* Great Expectations *with Dickens's earlier works, in terms of both 'art' and 'vision'; modern critics may look to make the comparisons on different grounds, but the same basic principle is invoked.*

*The popularity of this critical ploy is presumably evidence that
people – both critics and readers – find it useful and instructive. But, like
any approach, it has drawbacks if it is not handled sensitively and with
circumspection. For one thing it can be taken as implying that the author
behind the texts is more important than the texts themselves – a mysterious
but basically consistent personality offering glimpses of himself from work
to work (a residual Romantic notion). For another it can dispose the critic
to look for the similarities in a writer's works at the expense of real
differences: to put it another way, the individuality of texts is liable to be
sacrificed to a recognition of what they have in common. Finally, this
approach (more than most) has a tendency to devise clichés which are
appallingly difficult to shake off and which lazy critics are apt to construe
as revealed truth. The prevalent modern notions, for example, that the
early and late Donne have more in common than divides them, whereas the
early and late Dickens have more that divides them than holds them
together; these are truisms which by now obscure as much as they reveal.
They make the business of fresh, incisive criticism more difficult.*

Knowledge of at least the approximate date of our sonnet allows us to
consider it as a product of its age. We would be doing this, of course, if
we approached it via the Elizabethan sonnet sequence; but many other
options are open which are not tied to the generic form. We might
consider, for example, that most Elizabethan non-dramatic poetry was
written either by courtiers or by those vying for the patronage of
courtiers: in what ways might this affect its form and content? This
question has an equal appeal both to structuralists and to those who
value literature for its sidelights on social history. More generally, we
might appreciate that Elizabethan sonneteering is one manifestation of
the belated arrival of the literary Renaissance in England: in what other
ways does the sonnet reflect the intellectual climate of the time? Two
popular answers to this question have involved the investigation of
supposed free-thinking secret academies such as the Elizabethan Sir
Walter Raleigh's (c.1552–1618) 'School of Night' and the examination
of common themes and movements in literature and other arts,
particularly painting; may we usefully apply art terms, such as
Mannerism and Baroque, to the literature of the period?

We would probably rapidly discount the idea that our particular
sonnet refers in any way to public persons or events, but we could not
have done so if the selected passage had been a stanza, say, from
Spenser's *The Faerie Queene*: one strand of that poem's complex
allegory is a commentary on contemporary political and religious
events, while the whole is written in honour of Queen Elizabeth herself.
Clearly some literary texts need to be seen in relation to the ideas,
persons and events which would have been familiar to their original
readers, if we are to appreciate all their possible dimensions. (If you are a

New Critic, of course, such an idea is anathema: texts only mean what they mean *now*).

The New Critical caveat *about attempting to relate texts to their historical contexts is, in some respects, a salutary one; the danger of attempting to build a historical context for a piece of literature (as of biographical contexts) is that the evidence selected will be self-confirming and self-justifying, narrowing our response to the text rather than enlarging it. But to divorce literature entirely from the time in which it was written is to divorce it from many of the reasons why it is written and read. It is not easy to draw the line. On the one hand, we will surely miss much of the wit and pungency of Dryden's satirical poem 'Absalom and Achitophel' if we do not appreciate how aptly it relates to the Exclusion crisis of 1681; on the other, Pope's satire, 'The Rape of the Lock' remains extremely effective even if we know nothing of the loss of Miss Arabella Fermor's lock of hair which caused the poem to be written in the first place. Perhaps the difference will affect our view of the qualities of the respective works.*

In general terms we must beware of assuming that knowledge of the historical background or context can ever explain – much less explain away *– a particular text. If our knowledge that Dryden's Absalom represented the Duke of Monmouth, Achitophel the Earl of Shaftesbury and so on,* * *exhausted our appreciation of that text (explained it away, so to speak), we could conclude that it was a poor and unrewarding work. 'Absalom and Achitophel' has many other qualities – ones which some critics would appreciate as more purely 'literary'. Much of the value of the poem can be defined in terms of its blending of local historical material and wider literary concerns – the way the latter subsume and adapt the former. This, however, is a personal judgement – a way of balancing literature and its historical context. It will not be shared by, say, New Critics on the one hand or Marxists on the other. (See Part 2 for the reasons why.)*

The argument is not merely confined to works which relate, more or less directly, to historical events or social conditions (for example, social problem novels) but extends to the ways in which literary texts relate to intellectual controversies or, more generally, the history of ideas. Many Renaissance poems, for example, clearly allude to what Pope described as 'the Great Chain of Being' – a concept of the hierarchical interdependence of all things under God (see A. O. Lovejoy's great work on the subject, The Great Chain of Being, *1933); similarly, many late Victorian novels take sides in the general debate over Darwin's theory of evolution. As far as literary criticism is concerned, the crucial question must always be 'what*

---

*The original story of Absalom and Achitophel is in the Bible (2 Samuel 15–19). Dryden saw an analogy between it and contemporary events: his Absalom was the Duke of Monmouth (1649–85), eldest illegitimate son of Charles II, and his Achitophel was Anthony Ashley Cooper, Earl of Shaftesbury (1621–83), a leading politician opposed to the policies of the King and to the possible succession to the throne of James, Duke of York, the King's brother (who afterwards became James II).

does the author make of the idea/controversy?' It can never be sufficient, if our total task is the understanding and appreciation of a text, simply to identify an area of thought to which it alludes – to label it, for example, as Marxist, or absurdist, or Catholic or nihilist. We need to go beyond this and ask in what ways it is also literature.

It is for this reason – because the historical or intellectual context is irrelevant unless it furthers our understanding and appreciation of the text – that so far nothing has been said about the most notorious features of Shakespeare's sonnets: the fact that many (including our own No. 71) appear to have been addressed to a man (who may, or may not, have been the 'Mr. W. H.' referred to in the publisher's dedication of the 1609 text) and that the poet's relations with this man appear to have been complicated by the presence of a 'rival poet' and a 'dark lady' (to whom some of the later sonnets are clearly addressed). Contrary to many loudly-proclaimed assertions, we know nothing whatsoever about any of these characters, any or all of whom may have been real or fictitious, or about the circumstances which caused Shakespeare to write about them. It is a measure of human curiosity that so many *theories* about them have been put forward, and they may stand as a warning to all would-be critics. A whole string of eminent men, including Samuel Butler, Oscar Wilde, Leslie Hotson and A. L. Rowse, have made claims and assertions, none of which has met with general assent. The problem is that, in the absence of real corroborative evidence, it has been necessary for each scholar to apply quite disproportionate amounts of ingenuity and sheer guesswork to arrive at plausible conclusions. Their arguments will not be discussed here, but you would find it an instructive exercise to compare any two theories on, say, 'Mr. W. H.', noting just how much intelligence can be wasted on such questions as the dating and ordering of the sonnets, cryptic messages and covert allusions. A useful corrective to such impassioned speculations will be found in the dry scepticism of Samuel Schoenbaum's two books, *Shakespeare's Lives* (1970) and *William Shakespeare: A Documentary Life* (1975).

The real issue here is whether any of this has anything to do with literary criticism. It is not claimed that it would make *no* difference to our appreciation of Shakespeare's sonnets if we knew more for certain about the circumstances in which they were written, though there are those that would claim it, and they can be sympathised with. The totally disproportionate attention paid to such conjecture must be wrong inasmuch as it reflects a distorted attitude to what really matters about literature; to that extent it may be a useful object lesson for literary critics, helping us to fix our priorities. Such conjectures are not really interested in understanding and appreciating what has been written – the text; they regard the text only as a means to an end – a means of delving, all too often pruriently, for information about something else (be it Shakespeare's sexual habits, his social relations, the age he lived in, or whatever); they are all too often dedicated to 'proving' a preconceived notion rather than responding to the material given.

In each respect, the biographical furore over Shakespeare's sonnets (and like furores over the biographies of other major writers, though none is quite so tantalising as that of Shakespeare) is a useful reminder of the proper limits of literary criticism, which sets for itself the task of understanding and appreciating literary texts. It may employ one or more of many approaches and methodologies in this endeavour; it may adduce a wide range of information about the author, period or genre in this process. It may define and re-define theories of communication. But it must do so in ways that keep the text central – the end and not the means of the debate. Literary biography and the history of ideas are perfectly legitimate fields of study in their own right, and critics have much to learn from them. But literary criticism is quite large enough a subject in itself and has no need to go trespassing in other disciplines.

The critical essay

The first section of this Part has been concerned to sketch out the range of critical approaches available to anyone interested in coming to terms with a single literary text. Each carries with it (at least, in its purest form) a set of presuppositions about how literature 'works' and why it matters, but an open-minded critic should – with discretion – be able to draw on the insights of more than one approach, more than one methodology, in his own reading. The remainder of this Part will offer some advice on how the critic may go about the business of reducing his attempts to understand and appreciate the text to a comprehensible form: that of *the literary critical essay*.

We must firstly confront the general question of where his own essay will stand in relation to all those other essays and books of criticism that have gone before. Most teachers of literature regard the growing shelves of critical works in their libraries as something of a mixed blessing (even as they go on adding to them themselves). Will the students use them properly? The most obvious problem is simple *plagiarism*: the student cannot be bothered to write his own essay, so he copies something more or less verbatim from someone else's work on the subject and offers it as his own work. This is intellectual and academic dishonesty, and will be punished as such by a school or university. There are laws, of course, against actually publishing someone else's writing as if it were your own.

But simple plagiarism is, fortunately, rare. A much more pervasive problem derives from *the lazy use of critical books*: this is when the student makes only a half-hearted attempt at his assignment, never really understanding the text or the question he has been asked about it; so he reads a few critical works approximately on the question and finally cobbles something together, a string of second-hand ideas with no real thought of his own. This will certainly get the student low marks and little credit at his school or university. There is a further problem, which can be even more distressing in the long run: this is when a serious and dedicated student reads a work of criticism and finds it so compelling, so persuasive, that it totally supplants his own ideas: he can only see the topic of his assignment, perhaps of any assignment, through the eyes of a particular critic. This is not plagiarism; such a student usually makes no bones about his intellectual debts – it is hero-worship. It can be very exhilarating for a time, but hero-worship is really a symptom of dependency and arrested development and must not be encouraged.

All of these failings reflect a false sense of what criticism is, of why we read what other critics have written, and will inevitably result in bad essays from the student concerned. In the course of this book a large number of critical works have been mentioned and quite a few of them have been recommended; but in each case they have been recommended less for the opinions or attitudes they express (many of which the present author disagrees with) than for the way they have demonstrated a particular approach or methodology to the study of literature, a way of fusing their understanding and appreciation of texts, presenting this to fellow-readers in the shape of a reasoned argument. This is the business of criticism; this is what the student should be looking for when he reads other criticism; this is what he should be attempting to achieve when he writes his own essay. We look to other critics not for answers, for definitive readings (since no such thing exists), but for examples of how to reach our own answers, formulate our own questions.

Anyone engaged in writing a critical essay should therefore be aware that he is contributing to a long and continuing discussion, not only about one or two texts, but about literature in general. What makes his essay worthwhile is the fact that it is *his* contribution, not a pastiche of other people's. Once this is clear in his mind, the shape and scope of the essay should resolve themselves more easily and the technical requirements (such as footnotes and bibliography) should make ready sense.

The following observations are an attempt to reduce the principles and arguments advanced in this book to practical suggestions for your own essay-writing:

(1) Whenever possible, save the reading of other people's criticism until *after* you have thought through the question you have been set, or have set yourself, and until *after* you have read, preferably

more than once, the text or texts in question; start with your own understanding and appreciation – these are what count in the long run – however much you may hope to expand and refine them by referring to what other people have written; try to use reputable texts and observe the principles upon which they are based; keep notes at all stages of progress on what seems significant to you.

(2) When you do turn to what other people have written (there are few of us who will not benefit from doing so sensibly), do it with your eyes and mind open; use appropriate bibliographies and reference books to track down those works which will be most pertinent to your own chosen line of enquiry – be the master, not the slave, of that intimidating mass of criticism; look on the whole exercise as an aid and spur to your own thinking, not as a substitute for it; do not simply accept the other critic's judgements and conclusions but examine how he reached them; think of yourself as engaged in a civilised argument with him – your perceptions and standards against his; if it is not immediately obvious, ask yourself to what school he belongs – what methodology is he applying? What are his tacit assumptions about how literature 'works' and why it matters? Looking more closely at his argument – is there anything about the text/author/genre/period which might be relevant but which he has left out or skated over? Does he ignore particular characters, chapters, features of the vocabulary or imagery? Wherever possible, look for a second opinion, a different treatment of the same question (or, at least, a parallel question); are you still keeping notes?

(3) When you come to write your own essay, bear in mind that other people (for example, your teacher or tutor) will be asking the same questions of you that you were asking of the critics you read; they will not only want to know what your judgements and conclusions are – they will want to know how you reached them. What methodology have you used? What have you left out of the argument? You must not, therefore, simply make assertions and value-judgements – you must argue as logically and as clearly as you can for them, substantiating your case by detailed reference to the text, and to any other evidence you may draw upon, such as the author's sources, historical allusions, features of generic structure and so on; the more fully you demonstrate that you understand a text, the more weight your reader will attach to your appreciation of it. Bear in mind, however, that the most incisive observations about texts are not those which relate only to minor features but those which call attention to general or repeated characteristics, such as a thread of imagery or a narrative technique: you will only

clutter and slow down your argument if you record all examples of these – try to focus on the most typical, resonant or suggestive instances.

(4) Those reading your essay will look on it as part of the continuing discussion of literature; they will expect that you have compared your own reading of the text with those of other people, and they will expect you to acknowledge the fact at appropriate moments in your argument whether you quote directly from these other critics or not (it is, of course, quite valid to quote in moderation in order to demonstrate areas of common ground or disagreement; but try not to let such quotations clutter, disturb or dominate your own argument); it is probable that your school or university, or even any magazine for which you were writing, would prescribe for you the manner in which you should make such acknowledgements – perhaps by footnotes, perhaps by notes at the end of the essay; tastes vary in the style of these things: but the essential principle is the same in all cases – you should always give sufficient details of the books and essays you have been reading, down to the precise editions and pages, for another reader to be able to find and consult them, and make his own judgements; at the end of every essay you should *also* include a bibliography giving full details of *all* the books (texts, reference books, criticism) that you have used in the preparation of your essay, even those which you did not find particularly helpful and which you did not refer to directly; what you have read and rejected is often as informative – in the broad perspective of things – as what you have either accepted or seen fit to disagree with.

(5) If you appreciate that your essay is a small contribution to the long history of literary criticism, it may help you to keep a proper balance in terms of what you do and do not include; before you put pen to paper, you should broadly know what line of argument your understanding and appreciation of the text will lead you to follow (your notes should be useful here); you will do most justice to your own case and your readers' patience if you try to concentrate on that line of argument – to the exclusion of minor issues and incidental details, to the exclusion even of fruitful insights into the text which happen not to be germane to that argument; being able to make a coherent case counts more than being able to demonstrate your sensitivity – it distinguishes the person wishing to make a constructive contribution to the debate about literature from the confused and confusing hangers-on that all the arts attract: it demonstrates an awareness of, and a respect for, a reader who takes that debate seriously and is genuinely interested in what

you have to say; by the same token, a determination to stick to the
— point – to *your* point – is the best way of resisting the intimidating
presence of all that existing criticism: what you write may not be as
sophisticated, or knowledgeable, or suggestive as some other
criticism, but it will be *yours* and that is what makes it valuable; in
such a context, it should go without saying that you will not insult
your reader by telling him the obvious – that Shakespeare was a
genius, or Dickens wrote novels, that roses are red, or the sun
comes up every day: you are contributing to an adult debate and
may assume that your reader knows the text in question, and the
facts of life, at least as well as you do; so try not to waste time and
patience telling your reader who the characters are, what happens
in the plot, how many lines there are in a sonnet or what the
conventions of the epistolary novel are; get on with the
argument – *your* argument – and further your apprenticeship in the
mystery ('mystery = handicraft; craft, art; (one's) trade, profession,
or calling', O.E.D.) of literary criticism.

   For, to paraphrase Jonson on Shakespeare, a good critic's made,
as well as born.

Part 5

Suggestions for further reading

ABRAMS, M. H.: *The Mirror and the Lamp: Romantic Theory and the Critical Tradition*, Oxford University Press, London, 1953.

ATKINS, J. W. H.: *English Literary Criticism: the Medieval Phase*, Methuen, London, 1952.

ATKINS, J. W. H.: *English Literary Criticism: the Renascence*, Methuen, London, 1947.

ATKINS, J. W. H.: *English Literary Criticism: 17th and 18th Centuries*, Methuen, London, 1951.

AUERBACH, E.: *Mimesis: the Representation of Reality in Western Literature*, Doubleday, New York, 1957.

BATESON, F. W. and MESEROLE, H. T.: *A Guide to English and American Literature*, 3rd edn., Longman, London and New York, 1976.

ELIOT, T. S.: *Selected Essays*, 3rd edn., Faber & Faber, London, 1951.

ENRIGHT, D. J. and DE CHICKERA, E. (EDS.): *English Critical Texts: 16th to 20th Century*, Oxford University Press, London, 1962.

FRYE, N.: *Anatomy of Criticism: Four Essays*, Princeton University Press, Princeton, N.J., 1957; London, 1957.

FRYE, N.: *The Critical Path: an Essay on the Social Context of Literary Criticism*, Indiana University Press, Bloomington, 1971; London, 1971.

HALL, V.: *A Short History of Literary Criticism*, New York University Press, New York, 1963.

LODGE, D. (ED.): *Twentieth Century Literary Criticism: a Reader*, Longman, London, 1972; New York, 1972.

LOVEJOY, A. O.: *The Great Chain of Being*, Harvard University Press, Cambridge, Mass., 1936, London, 1936.

WATSON, G. (ED.): *The New Cambridge Bibliography of English Literature*, 5 vols., Cambridge University Press, London, 1969–77.

WATSON, G.: *The Literary Critics: a Study of English Descriptive Criticism*, 2nd edn., Woburn Press, London, 1973.

WATSON, G.: *The Discipline of English: a Guide to Critical Theory and Practice*, Macmillan, London, 1978.

WELLEK, R.: *A History of Modern Criticism: 1750–1950*, 4 vols., Cape, London, 1955–66.

WELLEK, R. and WARREN, A.: *Theory of Literature*, Penguin Books, Harmondsworth, 1970.

WIMSAII, W. K. and BROOKS, C.: *Literary Criticism: a Short History*, Routledge, London, 1957.

Index

CRITICS AND AUTHORS

Further titles

A DICTIONARY OF LITERARY TERMS
MARTIN GRAY

Over one thousand literary terms are dealt with in this Handbook, with definitions, explanations and examples. Entries range from general topics (comedy, epic, metre, romanticism) to more specific terms (acrostic, enjambment, malapropism, onomatopoeia) and specialist technical language (catalexis, deconstruction, *haiku*, paeon). In other words, this single, concise volume should meet the needs of anyone searching for clarification of terms found in the study of literature.

Martin Gray is Lecturer in English at the University of Stirling.

THE ENGLISH NOVEL
IAN MILLIGAN

This Handbook offers a study of the nature, developments and potential of one of the central features of English literature. It deals with the English novel from the historical, thematic and technical points of view, and discusses the various purposes of authors and the manner in which they achieve their effects, as well as the role of the reader. The aim is to bring to light the variety of options at the novelist's disposal and to enhance the reader's critical and interpretive skills – and pleasure.

Ian Milligan is Lecturer in English at the University of Stirling.

ENGLISH POETRY
CLIVE T. PROBYN

The first aim of this Handbook is to describe and explain the technical aspects of poetry – all those daunting features in poetry's armoury from metre, form and theme to the iamb, caesura, ictus and heptameter. The second aim is to show how these features have earned their place in the making of poetry and the way in which different eras have applied fresh techniques to achieve the effect desired. Thus the effectiveness of poetic expression is shown to be closely linked to the appropriateness of the technique employed, and in this way the author hopes the reader will gain not only a better understanding of the value of poetic technique, but also a better 'feel' for poetry as a whole.

Clive T. Probyn is Professor of English at Monash University, Victoria, Australia.

PREPARING FOR EXAMINATIONS IN ENGLISH LITERATURE
NEIL McEWAN

This Handbook is specifically designed for all students of English literature who are approaching those final months of revision before an examination. The purpose of the volume is to provide a sound background to the study of set books and topics, placing them within the context and perspective of their particular genres. The author also draws on his wide experience as a teacher of English both in England and abroad to give advice on approaches to study, essay writing, and examination techniques.

Neil McEwan is Lecturer in English at the University of Qatar.

ENGLISH USAGE
COLIN G. HEY

The correct and precise use of English is one of the keys to success in examinations. 'Compared with' or 'compared to'? 'Imply' or 'infer'? 'Principal' or 'principle'? Such questions may be traditional areas of doubt in daily conversation, but examiners do not take such a lenient view. The author deals with many of these tricky problems individually, but also shows that confidence in writing correct English comes with an understanding of how the English language has evolved, and of the logic behind grammatical structure, spelling and punctuation. The Handbook concludes with some samples of English prose which demonstrate the effectiveness and appeal of good English usage.

Colin G. Hey is a former Inspector of Schools in Birmingham and Chief Inspector of English with the Sudanese Ministry of Education.

READING THE SCREEN
An Introduction to Film Studies
JOHN IZOD

The world of cinema and television has become the focus of more an more literary work, and film studies is a fast-growing subject in schools and universities. The intention of this Handbook is to introduce the film viewer to the range of techniques available to the film maker for the transmission of his message, and to analyse the effects achieved by these techniques. This Handbook is geared in particular to students beginning a course in film studies – but it also has a great deal to offer any member of the film-going public who wishes to have a deeper understanding of the medium.

John Izod is Lecturer in Charge of Film and Media Studies at the University of Stirling.

The author of this Handbook

RICHARD DUTTON was educated at King's College, Cambridge, and the University of Nottingham. He taught at Wroxton College in Oxfordshire (a college of the Fairleigh Dickinson University, New Jersey, USA); since 1974 he has been a lecturer in English Literature at the University of Lancaster, where he is currently Chairman of the School of English. He has published several articles on Ben Jonson, John Bunyan and Charles Dickens; he has edited Jonson's *Epigrams* and *The Forest* and three volumes of *Jacobean Court Masques and Civic Pageants*. He is the author of *Ben Jonson: to the First Folio* (1983).